PRIMAL
STORYTELLING

MARKETING FOR HUMANS

ANTHONY L. BUTLER

LIONCREST
PUBLISHING

PRIMAL STORYTELLING
Marketing for Humans

FIRST EDITION

ISBN 978-1-5445-3425-1 *Hardcover*
978-1-5445-3426-8 *Paperback*
978-1-5445-3427-5 *Ebook*

CONTENTS

INTRODUCTION

I woke up to my mother's screams as she pulled my brothers and me out of bed. As I stepped into the hallway, I was paralyzed by the sight of flames rolling out of the ceiling, emitting thick smoke. A hungry, crackling roar filled the house. I was a little boy, and to my young mind, it was as if some mythical beast had broken through the chimney and was here to kill and eat us all. But it was that crackling sound that saved us when the chimney caught fire. The noise woke my mother up at the last possible moment, and we just managed to grab our coats and boots on our way outside, but nothing else.

Outside, it was bitter cold. The kind of cold that kills. It was deep winter in Western Montana and we lived outside of town. No one came to help. No firemen to put out the flames. No concerned neighbors. We lived in the wilderness, and we were on our own. We threw a few snowballs at the flames in frustration, but they melted before they hit anything.

Looking back, this was the first time I ever felt mortal fear.

Seeing the raging, uncontained fire was a primal moment. Losing everything was nothing. We were all alive! I actually felt relief after we were all outside and safe. I didn't realize it then, but it was also my first brush with the extremes of emotion and primal urges.

Years later, I commanded an infantry company during the invasion of Iraq, and my unit was one of the very first to fight its way into Baghdad, followed by months of house-to-house fighting in Fallujah, Iraq. War wears away at the civilized veneer we wrap our primal urges in during peacetime. Bearing witness to carnage and fear of death awakens our innermost primal survival instincts, and they are filled with both darkness and light. Men will perform great acts of bravery and sacrifice to protect their comrades, and some will also fall prey to their darker urges.

In a civilized society, surrounded by peace and the rule of law (for the most part), we bury our most terrible animalistic urges, but they are there. They are genetically coded. They are part of who we are and whether we are aware of them or not, they influence our every thought and action. We just don't notice them on a day-to-day basis.

My experience witnessing—and later studying and appealing to—primal urges and emotions in-depth uniquely positioned me to write this book. After I left the service and started my civilian career, the lessons of combat helped shape my thinking as a marketer. Many marketers are teaching their ideas on how to best reach an audience and influence them to buy something. Unfortunately, few of those methods tap into the power of storytelling or consider the primal urges and emotions of their audience. Case in point: as I told my story of my childhood home burning down in the midst of the bitter cold of a Montana winter, could you imagine the scene in your head and relate to the primal urge for survival? Humans love a good story; something about it resonates with our primal nature.

As I transitioned out of the military, I couldn't find a job back home in Montana. It was a tough search because there were few opportunities, and I didn't know what I wanted to do or how my skills from the military translated into the civilian world. To add to the pressure, my wife was pregnant with our first son, and we planned to shrink to a single income so she could stay home. As my transition date drew closer, I was forced to broaden my search, and at the last minute, I took a job in Connecticut at a manufacturing plant as a project manager. I thought it might be a good place to start to learn business, and it paid just about what I made in the military.

The job was interesting, and I loved the people I worked with, but I had made a real mistake. I underestimated the cost of living in Connecticut and the tax benefits of my military pay. I wasn't earning enough to support us, and after just a couple of months, we found ourselves in some financial trouble. We cut every corner we could to save money, but it just wasn't enough.

I had just started my first "real job" and starting a search for a new job that paid more didn't seem practical. I didn't have any definable skills or know what I wanted to do. My other choice was to find a second, part-time job, but I knew if I did that, I would never see my wife and new son. One of the reasons I got out of the military was to have more time for my family, and a second job didn't seem like a real choice.

Sometimes difficulty holds the seed to something better, and in this case, financial pressure and family considerations led me to decide to start my own business. It was one of the best decisions of my life and led me on an entrepreneurial journey. I started multiple companies, was part of a tech startup that went from zero dollars to hundreds of millions of dollars, and I served as the CEO of multiple companies. That choice helped me discover what I loved—helping businesses grow.

Today, I run a small business, Can-Do Ideas. The first part of its name is derived from the infantry company I commanded in Iraq. Our battalion motto was "Can-Do!" And the second part "Ideas" is because all great sales and marketing processes are built on great ideas.

Like all startups, we had our struggles the first couple of years, but we were profitable from day one. Then I started to notice something troubling. Our results weren't consistent. One content campaign might exceed expectations, but then the next one would fall flat, and it wasn't clear to me what was different between them.

We followed the same basic strategy for each campaign. We defined a buyer persona, brainstormed content, and then produced and published the content on our client's website and social media. We also included calls to action, lead magnets, and follow-up email campaigns. A fairly standard digital marketing mix for companies everywhere.

And then it happened. A fairly new client we had acquired chose to quit working with us before their contract was up. It was a bit of a shock. They told us the work was professional and they liked working with us, but they weren't getting any tangible results. We were doing the work, but it wasn't *working*.

It was a huge wake-up call for me. The inability to create results for clients is the death knell of an agency, and I didn't know what was wrong with our process. As far as I could tell, we were doing everything right. The creative was solid. We were publishing the right keywords. We were optimizing pages. We met our deadlines. Everything was technically correct, but something was off. There was a gap between our content development and the results we needed to produce. I reviewed everything we did, going back two years, but couldn't identify the issue.

Finally, feeling deeply frustrated and afraid my company might not survive, I signed up for a four-day business building forum in San Diego. I was looking for something to turn the business around, and during one of the sessions the speaker reminded us that "people make decisions emotionally and then justify them with logic." Decisions are an emotional process. The idea struck me. Think about the last time you took a second helping of lasagna or ate "just one more" cookie at the holiday party. You were trying to lose a little weight, but you worked out twice this week, so "you earned a treat," you tell yourself. The way that cheesy deliciousness or sugary-baked flour makes you feel is often more powerful than your logic. Another example of emotion-driven decisions can be found during car buying. Why do automakers put such an enormous emphasis on how cars look? Aren't they just a mode of transportation? The truth is, how a vehicle makes you feel is far more important to the sale than the gas mileage or newest safety features. It must first fit your mental picture of yourself before you will consider any logical notion of its function. After you decide it meets your emotional needs, you justify the decision with all the features and functions. And this same process takes place in almost every decision humans make.

The idea sent me into overdrive and I started researching everything I could about why people make decisions, and how emotions drive those decisions. That is when I stumbled on the idea of evolutionary psychology. Like many branches of science that study the human mind, evolutionary psychologists study emotions and urges, but they also study an unusual mental trait—the human obsession with stories. People are obsessed with stories, and much of our time is taken up with telling and consuming stories in different form. Scientists are unsure of the complete function of stories in the human psyche, but one thing is clear: they are an integral part of our human nature, and they help us connect with one another.

It was the final answer into what was not working in my agency. *We were writing for search engines and not for humans.* We were producing information with all the technical requirements of the day, but we missed the point entirely—the people. We needed to be creating for humans and not some bot. We needed to tell stories that touched on primal urges and emotions and do it in a way that would help brands grow. Primal urges are the vestiges of human instincts that are nearly extinct, but still influence human behavior.

I extended my research into literature and story structures. I explored the components that make a great story and developed a content creation framework that is not just for fiction but is for a brand creating content. After testing and improving the framework with multiple brands in both B-B and B-C businesses, *Primal Storytelling* emerged.

Primal Storytelling is the culmination of years of work and study of a single question, "How can marketers influence behavior?" I have tried to capture this system in an easy-to-follow process that any entrepreneur or marketer can use to create high-performing content. It is equally applicable in business to business (B-B), business to consumer (B-C), and even for account-based marketers. The process is not reliant on some new technology that will become obsolete in eighteen months, and I suspect it will stand the test of time. It is based on a deep understanding of human nature and storytelling, neither of which has changed in thousands of years. My hope is that *Primal Storytelling* will itself evolve and improve as Primal Storytellers worldwide work to create marketing for humans that connects and helps solve real problems.

I agree with Gary Vaynerchuk. People's attention is the most valuable commodity in the world. There are more than 1.5 billion websites globally, and the number of new daily posts on blogs and social media is staggering.[1] Many brands are struggling to cut through the noise and get noticed. They publish information on their website and social channels, but they fail to connect on a human level.

If you run a business or are responsible for marketing one, you may have noticed how difficult it is for a brand to produce high-performing content. The problem is many brands got the idea that to be relevant, they needed to "take part in the online conversation," and that meant publishing just about anything, no matter how vacuous. Most corporate content is a never-ending stream of online small talk where nothing of substance or value is ever really said. Low-quality brand content that rarely has a strategy behind it has become the default rather than the exception.

The result is that most brand content, especially from B-B brands, is low value and derivative of someone else's content. Or worse, it is pure clickbait trying to put someone into a sales funnel. Neither strategy works well long term, and most brands would be better off not publishing anything than publishing meaningless crap.

The book you're reading contains the entire *Primal Storytelling* system as well as examples on how to use it and questions to ask yourself as you create your own Primal Storytelling program for your company. If you would like to learn more about how to utilize the system as well as connect with other Primal Storytellers, navigate to www.primalstorytelling.com/bookresources.

CHAPTER ONE

THE BRAND DILEMMA

"At the center of every significant change in our lives today is a technology of some sort. Technology is humanity's accelerant."[1]

—THE INEVITABLE BY KEVIN KELLY

In 1988, I attended a family reunion for my great-grandfather, Charles Butler. It was his ninetieth birthday, and the party was held on the family ranch in Northern California. His father and uncle made the trek to California before the Gold Rush in the 1850s. They didn't have much luck finding gold, but they homesteaded about a thousand acres in the foothills of the Sierra Nevadas and turned it into a ranch. Charles was born in 1898. He was one of the last living pioneers.

He was born at home in a handmade wooden house, whose only luxuries were a hand-dug well and an outhouse. His life began with basically the same technologies available 2,000 years earlier during Roman times. At the party, he told us stories of how he used to cut firewood and haul it by horse and wagon to Sacramento to sell and how he and his father hunted elk all the way from the foothills to just outside of Sacramento. Today the stretch of I-80 where he pulled his wagon is paved over urban sprawl, and his favorite elk-hunting area has a nuclear power plant on it.

By 1988 his original farmhouse had almost caught up with the outside world. It had been upgraded with electricity, radio, television, indoor plumbing, and the telephone. He personally experienced the invention of industrialization, mass production of cars, nuclear weapons, airplanes, the computer revolution, the moon landing, and the space shuttle.

He also lived through the evolution of modern warfare, including two world wars, Vietnam, Korea, the first Gulf War, and many smaller conflicts. He was called for the draft during World War I, and ended up not serving because he was too old, but all five of his sons fought in World War II.

Fast forward fifteen years after the family reunion to 2003, and I was a captain commanding one of the lead infantry companies into Baghdad during the invasion of Iraq. The arsenal of technology available at the time of the invasion was amazing for its time: satellite imagery provided near real-time updates on the enemy; advanced radio encryption scrambled voice messages thousands of times a second and decrypted them at the receiving radio; and our sniper teams used thermal and infrared technologies to engage the enemy, who most of the time didn't even know we were there. During that time, attack-drone technologies were first tested on the battlefield—remotely controlled planes dropped bombs on enemy positions and engaged individuals. It was the beginning of drone warfare, which has the ability to strike anywhere at

ability to imagine the future. Our marvelous minds are able to think in possibilities, far beyond the present moment. It is a unique ability among all species on Earth.

But as much as we are different, we still carry the vestiges of our animalistic ancestry. Evolutionary instincts, such as the instinct to mate and care for our young, remain powerful driving forces in our behavior. Humans are able to overcome their instincts through their use of free will, but those instincts continue to help explain behavior.

Humans are also beset by a complex mix of emotions. These emotions influence every aspect of behavior and determine an individual's state of mind at any given moment, and state of mind determines action. Emotions seemingly defy logic, but they follow predictable patterns that, once understood, can help marketers in their quest to influence behavior.[5] I use the term "influence" deliberately. Long-term success in marketing requires that marketers avoid attempting to accomplish their goals through manipulation or propaganda, both of which are based on deception. Honesty must be a cornerstone and not an afterthought of campaigns. Deception may work in the short term, but the long-term consequences are destructive to building a brand. Think of all the stories you have heard of individuals who built stellar reputations over decades only to ruin them in an instant.

Humans are also social creatures. They long to be with and among others. In ancient times, being cast out from the Tribe was synonymous with a death sentence. In modern times, we have established that solitary confinement and isolation are not only unhealthy for individuals, but they can also lead to psychosis and death. Social considerations help explain much of human behavior. Seemingly small choices, such as what to wear on a daily basis or where to live contain underlying, and many times unconscious social influences. For a simplified way of describing social influences, I use the term "Tribe" to describe groups of people with demographic and/or psychographic similarities, but also to describe the deep connection an individual has with others. These individuals may or may not cluster together socially online or in person, but they may have deep patterns of similarities around interests, likes, fears, etc.

Marketers have long segmented audiences based on demographic traits, such as age, sex, and geography, but psychographic segmentation is much more nuanced and useful for content marketers than demographics alone. Determining and collecting psychographic data is more difficult and can require testing, analysis, and even some educated guesses, but is well worth the effort. Online companies are collecting and sharing an unprecedented amount of data, and it is a treasure trove of insights that can help lead marketers to a Tribal breakthrough in identifying a unique way to segment an audience.

The complexities of being human make it difficult to predict behavior on an individual basis. Each individual is unique. They have their own dispositions, views of the world, and interests. The nature and environment they are nurtured in from the time they are born until adulthood will form many of their choices and behaviors. But there are also commonalities among all humans that, if understood, can become powerful marketing tools.

Of the many influences on human behavior, marketers who

consider three driving forces of behavior will have an advantage: primal urges, emotions, and social influences.

- **Primal urges** as I described earlier are the remnants of our animalistic instincts. They are no longer behavioral blueprints but strong influencers of buying behavior.
- **Emotions** are how the mind feels about its circumstances, mood, or relationships and will often be the determining factor for decisions.
- **Social influences, or what I call Tribe,** is the social urge we all feel to connect with others individually and collectively. By understanding what makes humans, well, *human*, marketers are better able to connect and influence behavior.

Another quirk of humanity is Storytelling.[6] Stories are a big part of what makes us human. They have been around since humans were able to speak, and the oldest cave pictographs dating back more than 10,000 years seem to tell stories. Humanity's fascination with stories remains strong today. The next time you are at a party, wander around the room and notice how small clusters of people gather around while one person tells a story of some sort.

Stories help our minds retain information. Our minds think in images, and stories provide a framework for ordering images in a way that is easy to remember.[7] It is one of the reasons young children love stories so much. Through the stories, they absorb the nuances of language and learn about the world. When my oldest son was very small, *Shrek* came out on video. It is a great story with memorable characters, music, and a fast-moving plot. For months it was all he wanted to watch. It completely captivated him.

Marketers of the future must understand and recognize story structures and form. It is not optional if they want to be successful. It is also vital to understand the psychological factors that make a great story, touch audiences, and ultimately accomplish the real mission of every marketer, which is to inspire action that results in a sale. The point of brand marketing is not to tell great stories. Stories are the means to the end. They are the road to the goal that leads to connecting brands with their best-fit customers and motivates those customers to do business with you.

Marketers are not just passive storytellers. They are trying to convince audiences to spend their time, attention, and money on the goods and services that brands present. With the limitless possibilities of the internet, it has never been more difficult to garner attention and motivate action. But for those marketers who take on the challenge and learn the structures, story can be a powerful tool in the marketer's toolkit.

THE PRIMAL STORYTELLING FORMULA

There are billions of websites and hundreds of billions of new daily posts in the form of blogs, news feeds, videos, social media messages, advertisements, text messages, emails, etc., and determining how to stand out in the crowd is confusing and difficult. If you were to watch YouTube twenty-four hours a day, seven days a week, for the next eighty-two years, you would just barely finish watching all the new video content uploaded in the last hour.[8] And the online noise is only getting worse. What to do?

Most brand content is boring. It fails to deliver any insight or real value. Pick any industry and browse through company websites and you will see it, website after website publishing useless, and in many cases, nonsensical information. Their social media channels are even worse. The few brands attempting to connect on a human level to tell stories and provide any type of value are like an oasis in the desert—few and far between.

Marshall McLuhan was only partially right that "the medium is the message." In reality, the medium is not the message, but it affects the delivery of it. One of the biggest problems with the current state of media is that many brands are creating the messages *for* the medium itself. They are writing for search engines and social media algorithms. They want to trick these algorithms into calculating that their websites and social media channels are valuable and authoritative enough to deserve more attention. They have forgotten that real people are supposed to consume their content, and the result is millions of websites written in a way that no human would want to read.

It appears as if brand marketers realized they need to produce content but have no real idea how to do it, and they engage what I call "random acts of marketing." They hire an enthusiastic new graduate, give them the title marketing or social media coordinator, and send them out into the world to "be part of the conversation" and create content. Their team happily schedules dozens of social media posts, re-share others' content, post whimsical listicles, pithy quotes, and the news of the day, all in the name of contributing to the online world and trying to build an audience of some sort. But where is the connection with a real human?

Unfortunately, one of the most overlooked factors of brand marketing is storytelling, and a content marketing program that doesn't use stories is missing out on a powerful tool. Think back to all the commercials you watched during the last Super Bowl. Chances are the ones you remember told a story and evoked an emotional response, and the ones that fell flat just provided information and skipped the emotions.

Over and over again, I have heard from business owners and marketers and they have many of the same questions and fears about brand storytelling. They don't know how to create a brand story or what type of story to tell. One story is not enough. They need content for an entire year, and not just for a day or a week. How do they create storytelling content on an ongoing basis? It seems like a great dilemma.

The following four story structures (**Founding, Vision, Transformation, and Value** stories) were developed over the course of more than five years of testing and research. They work and can be deployed in nearly any industry. The first, three-story structures are nearly the same for every business, but the fourth structure has the potential to be wildly original, and your imagination and ability to execute the strategy will determine your success.

First is the company's **Founding Story**. It is similar to the superhero's origin story. It tells the tale of how the company started and, most importantly, why it was created and who it serves. Origin stories are designed to connect with an audience on an emotional level and show you have something in common. They also put a human face on the brand. The more affinity a story creates with an audience, the easier it will be to establish trust and credibility. The ideal is for the audience to think, "They are just like me."

The second brand story is the **Vision Story**. Why does the company continue to do what it does, and what is the big picture of what they are trying to accomplish? Audiences identify with vision. Think about Elon Musk's grand vision to help combat global warming by building affordable electric cars. Or to give humanity an alternate place to live by colonizing Mars. He created two grand visions that are much bigger than what the brands actually do, and they have driven enormous goodwill with audiences.

The third type of story is the **Transformation Story**. This type of story details a client's world before and after their encounter with your brand. They are success stories of problems being solved and dreams realized. They are always uplifting and positive and connect with the audience on an emotional and primal level. They are also the stories your sales team will tell as they are talking to new prospects. They highlight how working with your brand will help them succeed.

The fourth story type, and the one we will spend the most time focusing on, is the **Value Story**. This story is usually told in serial form with the customer as the main character. During this story, you are helping them solve a problem or transform themselves as part of a larger goal. It is the basis of a long-term nurture campaign that goes beyond the typical advertorial content and delivers insight and value long before a sale is ever made. A **Value Story** builds trust and relationship equity over time. Think of a **Value Story** as a foundation idea that weaves itself through everything you publish. It provides insight and draws the target audience back to your brand over a long period of time.

The four story types all have their uses within a brand's marketing mix and are not limited to written stories. They can encompass many formats, such as video, audio, blogs, white papers, and social media posts. The key is to create the underlying stories and tell and retell them until you hit on a storyline that resonates.

PRIMAL STORYTELLING IS A DELIBERATE PROCESS FOR CREATING STRATEGIC BRAND CONTENT.

Primal Storytelling is where social psychology, human emotion, and storytelling come together to create a story that connects with target audiences. The purpose of a primal story is to connect with the audience in an interesting and authentic way. It is at its core a methodology for understanding deeply who your real audience is and finding a way to deliver meaningful value that connects with them in a primal way. Once you understand the steps, you will be able to apply the process and build an audience in nearly any market.

The Primal Storytelling Formula:

Tribe + Urges and Emotions + Story = Primal Story

Following the process for each of the three pillars of a Primal Story can quickly build the foundation for creating powerful content that builds a relationship with your audience. I will cover this more in-depth in the "Primal Storytelling in Action" section later in the book.

Marketing communication follows technology, but the humans who marketers are communicating with do not intrinsically change over time. The amount of data on the internet is accelerating and it will become more difficult for brands to be noticed online. By paying close attention to the primal urges and emotions of their Tribe and utilizing age-old story structures, brands will improve their ability to connect and influence audiences. The *Primal Storytelling* formula is a tool to create high-performing content.

CAUTION

Guard against crossing the line between influence and manipulation. Although it may produce positive short-term results, the long-term consequences are dire. Honesty and authenticity are not just buzzwords. They are cornerstone virtues of marketers with a long view of their market.

KEY QUESTIONS

1. What stories does our brand already tell well, and how might we improve them by utilizing primal urges and emotions?
2. Of the four stories outlined in Chapter 1, which story is most important for our brand to develop and tell?
3. What do we already know about our Tribe that will help us identify their driving primal urges and emotions?

CHAPTER TWO

TRIBES

When Homo sapiens first emerged 70,000 years ago, compared to other animals, they were ill-equipped for survival. They were smaller and weaker than their close cousins, the Neanderthals. They lacked the physical strength of most predators and didn't have fangs, claws, or even a hide strong enough to protect their delicate skin from the elements.[1] There was no visible evidence that would have predicted the rise of Homo sapiens as the dominant species on Earth.

What wasn't visible was Homo sapiens' ability to think. Human brains are able to not only remember the past in great detail, but they can also ponder and plan for the future like no other animal. And as great as those two abilities are, their greatest gift of survival is more likely than not their ability to cooperate. What one person could never achieve, a group of cooperating humans can.

The development of sophisticated language made it possible for humans to send and receive information among members who gave the group the ability to coordinate actions like nothing the world had ever seen. Cooperation became the species' superpower. No individual human could match a saber-toothed tiger's strength and ferocity, but a group of humans with their tools and planning ability could easily hunt and kill a tiger. Most likely, their cooperation began in small family groups, and slowly developed into larger groups and eventually into tribes. For many thousands of years, humans primarily operated in small tribal groups, and early kingdoms were little more than collections of tribes whose leaders agreed to work together for mutual benefit.

Our ancestors' world was limited by the technology of their time. They only had access to the small group of individuals who were available in their physical world, and by the limitations of their minds to remember information about each of the individuals in their Tribe. Anthropologist Robin Dunbar hypothesized that early human tribes were limited to 150 individuals. It is the number of which an average human brain can maintain a relationship and remember.[2]

Before mass communication and rapid transportation, it was impossible to share an affinity with someone halfway across the world. All social connections were local because those were the only connections that existed. In some societies, travel outside of the local area was so difficult, generations of people lived and died without venturing more than a few miles from where they were born. The physical limitations of the world limited the types and number of connections a person could make.

Modern technology has changed everything about communication. Physical limitations no longer apply. We have extended our minds' capabilities with our technology, and our new ability to connect with like minds has become virtually unlimited. People from every corner of the world can connect in real time in almost anyway they want. Our limits are mostly defined by our own self-imposed ideas about connections and not technology. As an example, Taylor Swift has more than 300 million social media followers across Twitter, Instagram, Facebook, and YouTube. Her ability to interact with her "tribe" is unprecedented in human history. In just a few moments, she can post a written message, audio, or video and instantly broadcast it to all of her followers, and they can answer her in real time.

What hasn't changed with the technology is our deep need to connect with others. Relationship management became as much of a survival skill as being able to detect a dangerous predator in the area. Mothers needed help in raising their young. Hunters needed help coordinating their hunts. Labor was shared, and everyone benefited. Banishment from the Tribe was the most terrible of proclamations. It more likely than not was a death sentence unless an individual could be quickly adopted into another band. Long-term survival alone was just not possible.

Our need for social contact is more than just a pragmatic choice of survival. It is such a deeply ingrained need that when deprived of all human contact, humans quickly begin to experience mental problems and, in extreme cases, lose their sanity. Prisoners kept in isolation develop mental problems, such as hallucinations, depression, confusion, and lethargy and are often driven toward self-harm, such as cutting and ultimately, suicide.[3] Suicide among inmates in solitary confinement is five times higher than the general prison population, and that includes when precautions against suicide are taken with isolated prisoners. Even when isolation does not include sensory deprivation, the isolation from others causes harm, and the United Nations has categorized long-term solitary confinement as torture and banned its use.

By geologic standards of time, where change is measured in hundreds of thousands or even millions of years, the technologies allowing mass connection happened half a second ago. Gutenberg's invention of the printing press in 1439 was the start of mass communication. It led to accelerating the spread of ideas through mass-produced books and led to a surge in worldwide literacy. The next big leap started when Alexander Graham Bell took out the first US patent for a telephone in 1874. But the telephone wasn't widely used in the US until after World War I. The radio, the first mass-market medium of electronic communication, didn't become popular until the 1920s and was followed by the rise of television in the 1940s. But each of these mediums, print, telephone, radio, and television, were primarily one-to-many models, a central station broadcast to the masses.

The rise of the internet in the 1990s combined audio and visual mediums of communication and facilitated one-to-many and many-to-one communication. No longer does all communication filter through a central facility that controls the message. Individuals have the ability to message and connect with others on a personal level instantaneously. The internet democratized mass communication, and it changed the way we think of tribes by making our ability to connect nearly infinite. Loose connections among a group that closely identifies with one another are now possible.

For marketers, and for the *Primal Storytelling* system, the term "Tribe" means something different than it meant to our ancestors. A Tribe is no longer a local phenomenon limited by the bounds of family groups with social, political, racial, or religious connections, although it can still contain those attributes. A Tribe is a target group that can be identified through a demographic or psychographic commonality, such as gender, age, geography, or by a more subtle connection, such as interest, cause, or idea. The individuals within the Tribe may or may not have a self-identity as a member of the group. For example, football fans may have an awareness of their group identity and affinity for other members who root for the same team, whereas new mothers may be targeted as a group, but they don't usually identify themselves as part of a larger group.

A TRIBE IS ANY GROUP OF PEOPLE
WHO CAN BE IDENTIFIED AND
TARGETED THROUGH DEMOGRAPHIC OR
PSYCHOGRAPHIC CHARACTERISTICS.

Creating a "persona" to visualize who you are marketing to can be very helpful when developing content. A persona is a fictional representation of an individual within a Tribe. They encapsulate the primary traits of the Tribe.

A self-identifying Tribe will often have important relationships with members of the group, such as a church or sports team. And, beyond pure survival, membership can deliver many individual benefits, such as feelings of security, belonging, status, and even love.

Tribes can take many forms, such as the traditional idea of family units with a mother, father, and their children, as well as extended family, to less formal groups, such as sports teams, interest groups, and military units. Tribes can form around any common interest, demographic, or even an idea. For example, Boston Red Sox fans, new moms, and foodies are all examples of Tribes. Each is an identifiable group bound together by a demographic or psychographic commonality.

Many times, Tribes occur on their own as a natural outgrowth of shared interests and demographic commonalities, or they can be strategically formed. The goal of a planned Tribe is to indoctrinate new members into the culture of the group, and then focus them on the purpose of the Tribe. Tech entrepreneurs, drill sergeants, and cult leaders all strive for the same thing. They want to instill a sense of belonging within the Tribe as quickly as possible and help individuals think of themselves as part of a group and movement bigger than themselves. Members who integrate well help the group achieve its goals, and they spread the word and begin recruiting others into the group. They become evangelists for their Tribe because, as we will see in the next section, one of the overarching needs of every Tribe is to grow.

Establishing a deep sense of belonging is the holy grail for marketers. Belonging extends far beyond the vagaries of brand loyalty, and helps individuals begin to identify themselves as part of something, and it could have a lot to do with a product or service.

Think about Harley Davidson motorcycles. To be part of the Harley Tribe, you have to own a Harley, which is an incredible boon for the brand. Within the Harley Tribe, other motorcycle brands are looked down upon, and individuals who own other brands and not a Harley are certainly not part of the Harley Tribe. It is a singular distinction of the Harley Tribe. Thousands of Harley Davidson clubs have sprung up around the country, completely separate from the company, but to the company's benefit.

Harley owners exude independence and a rebel attitude. They embody freedom, resilience, and a type of hardworking fun that is contagious. There is such an emotional connection to the Harley Tribe that members are often members for life. How many brands can boast such customer affinity that customers get tattoos that include the company's logo and name?

In 2006, Fred Reichheld published his groundbreaking book, *The Ultimate Question.*[4] He detailed what came to be known as the Net Promoter Score (NPS) methodology. Simply put, NPS is a way for brands to measure customer satisfaction. What is interesting are the types of relationships brands at the top of the NPS scale, such as Harley Davidson and Apple, and brands at the bottom of the scale have with their customers. Brands at the highest levels of NPS invariably have identified Tribes of people and built a tight relationship with them. At the very highest level, they have created a new Tribe that is built around the brand.

TRIBAL CHARACTERISTICS

All Tribes have their own language. It is one of the few commonalities among groups. Communication evolves as an outgrowth of the interests and experiences of the group. It reflects their collective personality and helps unite them.

For example, in the past few years, the internet has exploded with mommy bloggers. These are women who are by and large young mothers who begin to write about their experiences as mothers. They will often share what is working for them and provide information on different topics that may help make other mothers' lives easier. And within the mommy bloggers, small micro-Tribes develop.

There are dozens of categories by psychographic topics, such as healthy eating, gluten-free, playtime, vaccinations, learning, breastfeeding, ADHD, etc. Any one of these groups can form a micro-Tribe, and as a quick search will tell you, they have a vast and active following. As a demographic, the groups are primarily mothers in their early twenties to late thirties who share common interests related to their children.

Another example of a micro-Tribe is sports enthusiasts of all kinds. Sports like football, Indy racing, mixed martial arts, and golf all have millions of avid followers who have their own unique language, culture, and customs. The language of a micro-Tribe can be so specialized that it is not unusual for an outsider who is listening to a conversation by tribal members to barely understand what they are talking about. Within the micro-Tribes, they have demographic trends, but the unifying feature of the Tribe is psychographic in nature.

TRIBES DEMAND GROWTH

The great Roman emperor Marcus Aurelius and American president Abraham Lincoln have much in common. They both led their countries during painful, destructive civil wars, and worked tirelessly to hold their nations together. Their main goal was to maintain the territorial boundaries of their countries and protect the people who lived within those borders, even though vast cultural differences existed across all the people they ruled.

The cultural differences between the US northern and southern states were more than just a disagreement over slavery. There was a wide gulf in outlook on states' rights, the role of the federal government, religious practices, and many social differences between the two groups. To varying degrees, state citizens thought of their state as a country that was also part of the coalition "the United States of America."

Under Marcus Aurelius, the Romans ruled a wide variety of cultures who spoke different languages and even worshipped completely different gods. For example, the Romans and Egyptians could hardly have been more different, and yet under Aurelius, the Egyptians became part of the Roman Empire. The only common bond holding Rome and Egypt together was military force, and in later years, as the empire fragmented, Egypt, along with most other provinces, broke away from Rome.

Economic and security considerations certainly drove some of the decision-makings of both rulers. Controlling land and resources is an important aspect of building a thriving economy and keeping enemies at bay. The southern succession would have meant giving up vast swaths of land and coastline, and the "Pax Romana," the peace that existed among the cultures ruled by the Romans stretched across the entire Mediterranean. But there was also another force that drove both leaders.

Allowing the Tribe to shrink is almost unthinkable. Growth is the default focus for tribes, or in this case, nations, of all sizes.

The unspoken rule is to never allow the Tribe to shrink. Growth is power. To members, growth is a sign of health, and it can be a signal that the cause of the Tribe is righteous. Tribes that shrink lose power, and if the loss of members becomes too great, they eventually cease to exist. It helps explain why countries will fight so acrimoniously for even the tiniest swaths of land around the world. It is also one of the reasons why leaving a Tribe is so difficult. Leaving means renouncing social ties to a large group. The remaining members may become enemies, and losing relationships is difficult for the departing members.

Departing a Tribe can be a traumatic experience, and society at every level frowns upon leaving. For instance, renouncing the citizenship of your birth is fairly rare. Only a small number of people undertake it on a yearly basis. And world governments require anyone who renounces their citizenship to take up citizenship elsewhere. Human society does not allow individuals to not be a part of a recognized national government. Tribal power at the national level is, for all intents, unlimited. The social structures, borders, and laws, although all imaginary, are mandatory constructs, and anyone who attempts to disregard the system is subject to harsh penalties and repercussions up to and including the death penalty.

At the micro-level, the collective human Tribe frowns on members who opt-out of membership. It is why many cult members find it so difficult to leave their cult. They are not just leaving an idea; they are severing personal ties and relationships. The sense of belonging that comes with a social structure is a powerful force that cannot be underestimated.

Lincoln could have made the choice to allow the southern states to secede, just as Marcus Aurelius could have decided to stop expanding the Roman Empire and allow some of the outer regions to become separate countries. They both could have attempted to maintain what they had through other means, but consciously choosing to shrink the Tribe goes against a natural tendency built into human nature.

In the 1980s and early 1990s, Mikhail Gorbachev oversaw the dissolution of the Soviet Union. Since the end of World War II, Russia had overseen an empire that, similar to the Roman Empire, unified many different cultures and countries across vast territories. His example of consciously choosing to shrink an empire stands nearly alone in history. His idealistic vision that dismantling the Soviet Union would usher in peace and prosperity was not shared by many citizens of the Soviet Union. In Russia, Gorbachev's native country, Gorbachev is reviled as a traitor for betraying the ideals of the Soviet Union and the fall of Russia as a great power. He was forced to leave Russia and now resides in the United States, where more people share his vision of the world.

Below the national level, Tribes don't hold the same power, but they maintain some of the same social power as a nation. Micro-Tribes are always focused on maintaining and growing membership and leaving it is difficult. Whether a Tribe is a small business running a tight-knit community of customers with some sort of commonality, a social club, church, martial arts studio, or just a group of hobbyists, there will be social aspects that help hold everyone together.

Even when growth doesn't make a lot of sense, there is almost always a push to expand membership or to do more to maintain the interest of members. The push is to improve social interactions and create a growing entity. To stop growing is to begin to decline and die.

Humans are loss averse. Once we have something, we will go to great lengths to keep it. Loss aversion is part of what makes leaving a group so difficult. The thought of losing status, social ties, and their benefits to our self-esteem is a real consideration that will keep a member in a Tribe for far longer than they may have otherwise intended. If you have ever been a member of a tight-knit martial arts school, you may have observed that many members will only train occasionally and will go long periods without training at all but will maintain their membership. Leaving is hard, even when the activity no longer holds their interest or is deeply fulfilling for them. Their social ties with other members of the gym hold them there.

SOCIAL PRESSURE IS POWERFUL

In ancient times, strangers from outside the Tribe were an unknown danger and treated with caution. Intertribal violence was something to fear and came with dire consequences. It is one of the reasons so many children's fairy tales revolve around the theme of "stranger danger." And it helps explain why testimonials are so effective at driving sales. When others of the same group accept a stranger, they are, in a sense vouching for them and letting the rest of the group know they are safe and not a threat.

Social psychologists have identified a phenomenon termed the **bandwagon effect**, which is a powerful form of social pressure. It is a major motivating force that, when used as a deliberate marketing strategy, can amplify the results of campaigns.

The bandwagon is a nod to an early nineteenth-century phenomenon of a parade wagon that hosted a band. The band would play music and encourage people to jump aboard and enjoy the music while it moved forward.[5] Modern use of the term describes the tendency of groups of people to notice the behavior of others and to "jump on the bandwagon" with them. In other words, to mimic them and do what they are doing to be part of the crowd. There are many such examples of the phenomenon throughout history, from wearing hats to smoking to owning certain electronic devices.

Adoption of the Apple iPod is a more recent and larger example of the bandwagon effect. Apple didn't invent the MP3 player. In fact, they were a couple of years behind the competition when they first released the iPod. But Apple had something most other companies of that time did not have. They had a Tribe of distinct followers who identified themselves as the "think different" crowd.[6]

Apple released the iPod on October 23, 2001, and first-year sales were anemic but escalated year over year.[7]

December 2001: 25,000
January 2003: 600,000
January 2004: 2 million
December 2004: 10 million
January 2006: 42 million
April 2007: 100 million
April 2008: 152 million

September 2009: 220 million
September 2010: 275 million

Owning an iPod became a powerful social signal, and the more people who owned one, the more people who wanted one. It became as much of a cultural phenomenon as it was the need to listen to music. There were many alternatives to the Apple iPod on the market that were cheaper and arguably just as good, but iPod grabbed the lion's share of the market. The bandwagon effect is real, and it can move entire markets when activated.

Kevin Kelly, the founder of *Wired* magazine, wrote an essay in 2008 called "1,000 True Fans."[8] He makes the argument that creators with "true fans," defined as people who love your work so much that they will buy nearly anything you produce, can make a living with as few as 1,000 fans. Apple had far more than just 1,000 true fans. They had a Tribe of hundreds of thousands who loved Apple, and over the next two years, many of them rushed to buy the iPod.

As Apple's fans bought the iPod and raved about it to their friends, both in person and online, it became a sort of social phenomenon. The more people bought it, the more it was seen, and the faster sales accelerated. If you look at the sales numbers, after December 2004, sales reached a nearly unprecedented volume. It was the bandwagon effect in full effect.

The bandwagon effect is a type of social proof, and it is another reason, along with the aforementioned social acceptance, that also helps explain why customer testimonials are effective in helping to improve sales. The direction of the group is so important to the individual that it is very difficult for an individual to disregard social proof. What other people do and believe has real power to persuade on the individual level.

For brand marketers, making an inroad with a Tribe must begin with building social proof that can be used to persuade and encourage other Tribe members to "jump on the bandwagon." Appealing to logic will have far less effect than helping them understand that "everyone else" is doing it, too. The more you can make your brand seem ubiquitous, the more likely it will actually become ubiquitous. The fear of missing out (FOMO) is a real phenomenon and has its roots in the primal need for Tribe. If everyone is doing it, I better do it, too, if I want to continue to be a member of the Tribe.

The 2014 "Ice Bucket" challenge was an online fundraiser that raised more than fifty million dollars for ALS in one month and is a prime example of the bandwagon effect. The challenge entailed making a video of yourself dumping a bucket of ice water over your own head and then tagging additional people in your network to also take the challenge and to donate to ALS. Many people who took the challenge had no idea what ALS even was, did not donate, but they did it to be part of the crowd. They didn't want to miss out on the fun.

TRIBAL DATA: YOUR MOST VALUABLE ASSET

Data may be the most valuable resource in the world today. It drives billions of dollars in revenue. Just Google and Facebook, who are two of the largest data brokers in the world, are doing more than $150 billion in revenue a year. They are unique in the world because their entire value proposition to the marketplace is user-supplied data that they resell. Yes, they both provide a service that is valuable to the users, but neither makes their money through their service. They make their money selling access to the data they collect.

The idea of big data is exciting, and if you read the headlines trumpeting the arrival of "The Age of Big Data," you would think every business must be using data to predict customer behaviors and craft compelling offers. But the reality is most companies are still just winging it. They are going to market based on the gut feelings of the executive team or maybe a visionary founder. Very few companies are marketing using data, and it might be one of the most powerful processes a company can develop to garner a competitive advantage in the marketplace.

Target is famous or, depending on your perspective, infamous, for their ability to gather and use data to profile customers and target them with relevant messages. In his landmark 2012 article, "How Companies Learn Your Secrets," Charles Duhigg tells the story of how Target was able to determine a teenage girl was pregnant just based on her pattern of browsing the store she visited—even before her father knew she was pregnant.[9] Target used motion sensors and internet-enabled microchips placed throughout the store that timed how long she spent looking at certain items to create a probability that she was more likely to be pregnant. They then used the determination to follow up with her by mailing her print advertisements and coupons for baby-related items.

Marketing with data is vital to be competitive. You must get beyond just what your gut tells you about your target market, or you will be stuck in the mass-market puzzle, and not know exactly who is receiving your messages. Traditional advertising such as TV, radio, and print media is more expensive and less effective than ever, because it is sending broad messages to the masses instead of targeted messages. The cost per lead skyrockets when you have to send the messages to nearly everyone. And people are so overwhelmed with the constant barrage of marketing messages that unless a message is about something they are actively seeking, they will just tune it out. Getting noticed is harder than ever before, and it is vital that every piece of content you produce is narrowly targeted, or consumers will just ignore it.

The answer to a noisy and overly crowded market is to stop trying to market to the entire world. Focus all your resources on the few, best-fit clients. Learn everything possible about them and develop content that is so valuable and interesting for them that they cannot help but find your content and eagerly consume it and, in the process, find you and your wonderful company.

Niche groups form communities. For example, the Jiu-Jitsu community is very small. It is a subset of sports enthusiasts and martial arts practitioners. It has its own language, customs, and norms that are very different from any other group. Imagine how expensive it would be to market to this group using mass-market methodologies. You could run TV and radio ads, and you might net a few, but the large majority of your money would be wasted on people who don't care about Jiu-Jitsu.

Gathering microdata will paint a broad picture of a single individual or persona. It should be detailed enough to allow your team to craft content that seems as if it was written for a single person. When they read it, they should feel as if you wrote it just for them. When you can get that narrow with your content, it will have a much more powerful ability to inspire them to take action.

When a contact first visits your website, there are a number of key questions the marketing team must ask: Who are they?, What problem are they trying to solve?, What does this prospect already know about us?, and What do they already know about the solution we offer?

These questions drive the content you prepare for them, the questions you ask on your forms, and they will dictate all of your follow-ups. But before you can begin finding the answers, it is important to map out the entire content process. To simplify the process, I borrowed a technique from the military called "backward planning." I will discuss this more in the dedicated section in the chapter on the Art of Marketing, but essentially, backward planning helps planners design a framework around their ideas. They envision an objective and begin asking the question, "What important action must occur just before this outcome, and what is required to make it successful?" They continue asking the question until they have identified all the significant actions that must take place and the resource requirements from the beginning to the end of the mission.

For marketers trying to make sense of their marketing funnel, backward planning begins at the most important action you want a contact to take at the very end of the funnel—the last step. It is usually to buy something, book an appointment with the sales team, or some other important action.

What had to take place just before they got to this step to inspire them to get here? Maybe they attended a webinar, clicked through from an email sequence, or took action from another offer they had. Then ask the other three questions:

1. Who are they?
2. What problem are they trying to solve?
3. What do they know about us?

The questions will focus your efforts and help clarify your thinking. The first sequences may not work as well as you like, but by continuously reviewing the results of your pages, and testing different offers, you will eventually hit a breakthrough and a process that works for your business. Once you know who they are and the problem they are trying to solve, it becomes much easier to test content that will move them forward in your funnel.

The third question, "What do they know about us?" is more difficult to learn from them. You cannot assume they read your About Us page or even browsed your website, and it will be important to sprinkle in credibility factors from the beginning. Credibility factors come in many forms, such as testimonials, awards, certifications, and even the look and feel of your website can make a difference.

DEMOGRAPHIC AND PSYCHOGRAPHIC DATA

There are two types of data to collect—demographic and psychographic data. The first type of data and the one most marketers are already familiar with is **demographic data**, such as age, job title, industry, income, location, sex, etc. It helps narrow down the entire population of the world into a more defined group with unique characteristics, and answers the first question, "Who are they?" Demographic data is fairly straightforward to collect, and in many cases, you can purchase it from data brokers cheaply. Demographic data helps segment your contacts, but it is rarely enough to build the foundation of a breakthrough campaign.

The second kind of data is **psychographic data**. It is more valuable than demographic data and harder to gather. Psychographic data is internal to the individual. What are their preferences? What are they afraid of when it comes to doing business with you? What motivates them? Besides the most obvious benefits, is there something they appreciate about your company's offering? Is there something personal to them that should be considered?

As an example, a CEO might want to implement a new marketing automation system into his company, not just to scale marketing, but to show he is focused on innovation and has a vision for the future. If this were true, you could then focus on developing content that talks about how HubSpot is far ahead of the rest of the market and has a technical road map that is far-reaching and focused on the future. These are all intangible elements of the sale that are important to only one persona— the CEO.

Psychographic data tends to be less concrete and more personal to individuals but can still be categorized across a niche group of individuals. For instance, people who played hockey as a kid are much more likely to love hockey as adults. "Hockey lover" is a bit of psychographic data that could apply to an individual or a group, and it could be used to target them in a way that you couldn't if you just had a list of everyone in the world who loved sports.

Another example of a psychographic element can be found in the luxury market. How does a purchase make an individual feel? A $20,000 Rolex watch will, in all likelihood, keep good time, but that is unlikely the only reason someone buys a Rolex. The Rolex brand is also a status symbol. It has cultural value and may help the individual feel accomplished, important, or even successful.

I have done a great deal of work in technology markets, such as software as a service (SaaS), IT services, and IT support, and I identified three different personas that often play a role in purchasing decisions—the office manager, CFO, and the in-house IT manager. Their psychographic reasons for buying or not buying a product or service are vital to the sales and content development process.

For instance, the office manager is often worried about being assigned work that she doesn't understand. She is usually nontechnical and will quickly become frustrated with anything she doesn't understand. Changing the messaging to her to focus on how easy it would be to work with you and avoiding any type of technical jargon will go a long way toward removing her resistance.

The second persona, often at the exact same company, is the financial manager or CFO. They often get involved in IT decisions and don't care much about how hard it will be to work with a solution. They are completely focused on ensuring the service is a good value and if it will prepare them to pass an IT audit.

The third persona is the IT personnel. They were often concerned about whether or not they were going to lose their jobs or if a portion of their responsibilities would be outsourced. They would often ask questions trying to understand the underlying intent of the engagement far before they could focus on what we were actually offering.

By gathering data on the three personas, we were able to tailor our marketing material for each of them to address what was most important to them as individuals. It worked wonders.

Most B-B companies focus on surface-level demographic data, such as first name, last name, email, title, company, phone number, address, company size, and industry. These data points have value, but they will not help your team develop enough insight into the buyer's persona to create extraordinarily interesting and engaging content.

DEFINE THE TARGET AND GET PERSONAL

Before the Army shoots a missile at a target, they gather as much intelligence as possible on the target and answer a series of key questions such as, "Is the target above ground or below? What is the target made of? Does it need to be completely destroyed or just disabled?" The answers to the questions determine the ammunition, size, and type of missile fired.

Marketers must look deeply at their target markets and assess who they are as people. They must develop a profile that includes personality traits, goals, fears, beliefs, and more—anything that separates them from the rest of the human race that is important. Always remember, companies, even giant Fortune

1000 companies, never buy anything. Individuals within these companies make the buying decisions, and they are real-life human beings who have their own personal inclinations that may or may not be rational and, more likely than not, are emotional. If you can garner a deep psychographic insight into their emotional makeup or behavior, it can change everything for your marketing campaigns.

Charles Duhigg, in his book, *The Power of Habit*, tells the story of how when Proctor and Gamble (P&G) first introduced Febreze to the market, it failed miserably.[10] No one wanted another product to kill smells. People who are constantly exposed to bad smells, over time, adapt to the smell until they don't notice it anymore. It wasn't until they learned something special about their target market—housewives—that they were able to make a breakthrough. After conducting intensive research, they noticed many mothers who were cleaning the rooms of their children, would pause to look at their work one last time and smile just before departing the room. They interviewed many women and learned that it was their way of taking a moment to celebrate a job well done. They had a psychographic urge to do a good job for their family and wanted to celebrate it. This seemingly tiny insight into the behavior of women changed P&G's entire approach to their marketing. They refocused their campaign on encouraging mothers to celebrate a job well done. P&G went on to sell more than $230 million Febreze products in the year after their relaunch.

PERSONAS

In determining what data to collect, start by creating a rough profile of the target persona. It is more important to focus on the general makeup of the profile than agonizing over getting every detail correct. For instance, if women are represented in disproportionate numbers, but you don't know the actual percentage, just choose a number that will give the team the right idea. Saying 90 percent are women versus 75 percent has no real value. The majority of the demographic are still women and will be the primary focus.

Below are two rough profiles as examples—a financial professional and an office manager. They were prepared for technology marketers who were applying the inbound methodology in their markets. The first profile was created strictly from a couple of quick online searches and basic knowledge of financial professionals. The second profile on office managers was created after meeting with dozens of office managers in multiple industries, listening deeply, and observing the behavior of office managers during the sales process. Neither persona profile is exact, but both contain important information to help guide the marketing department in developing the right editorial voice and content that will appeal to the target audience.

Financial Professional: Titles, such as CFO or Director of Finance. Tend to be 90 percent or more male who are college educated. The average age of a CFO in the US is fifty-three. They are worried that they do not know enough to properly manage their IT systems and personnel. Few undergraduate and graduate programs included IT management as part of the curriculum, and many financial professionals graduated from college more than twenty years ago. They are learning IT management through self-study. Their need to understand, focus on controlling costs, and achieving compliance are common themes.

Office Managers: They are primarily female, age twenty-five to sixty-five-plus. Most have a college degree, with around 20 percent having just high school, an associate degree, or some college. Office managers tend to be information gatherers who can say no to a provider but do not normally have the ability to make a hiring decision alone. They are key influencers in deals but have a very different perspective than CEOs, CFOs, or financial professionals.

Almost all their questions during the sales process revolve around granular implementation details and the day-to-day relationship management of services. They are normally nontechnical and will often utilize passive-aggressive tactics to influence the process. Many will resist change at all costs, especially if they already have established relationships. One of their main fears is to be embarrassed by not understanding something, and it is important to avoid technical jargon without being condescending. They are also often worried if a new service will increase their workload.

If you have demographic details of your contacts, but not psychographic data, spend some time brainstorming how you will collect it. Surveys, interviews, focus groups, and your sales team are all good ways to get started.

WHAT DATA IS IMPORTANT?

Determining what data is important is not easy. On the surface, it seems simple. Just narrow down the market: segment targets by individual demographic points, such as company size, industry, and job title. Maybe those are the types of companies who buy from us most, or they are the type of people who buy from us. Or if a company is conducting B-C marketing, they might try to narrow down their market by:

- Gender
- Interests
- Age
- Income levels

The problem is one or two data points can't tell you enough of their story to be meaningful. There are more than 325 million people and twenty-eight million businesses in the United States alone.[11] It is a vast market with enormous variety. You don't have enough money or time to try to market to them all. You have to be much more specific with the data.

For B-B marketers, company size, industry, and job title will get you part of the way, but the hard part comes next. Why are they buying? What draws their interest to your specific product or service? It will almost always be a psychographic data point that ties the story of your target market together.

Back to the IT services analogy from before. Most IT companies love to target financial professionals such as the CFO, and many will go to great lengths to acquire lists of CFOs so they can market to them in hopes of getting a meeting to talk about managed services. But one data point is just not enough information to run a successful campaign. How large are the companies you are targeting? If they are Fortune 500 companies and your IT services firm is only three people, it is probably not a good fit. What is their industry? Is there any specialized language? Are there any commonalities among groups that you work best with?

A much better profile might be:

- The CFO of a mid-sized law firm
- Does not have a head of IT
- Has multiple offices in different locations

It is three separate data points that when taken together, paint a much more powerful picture of the target. Who this data excludes is as important as who it includes. It excludes the smallest law firms. It also excludes firms who have a head of IT who might be difficult to deal with and who is insecure and sees your firm as a threat to their business.

Now add a psychographic data point and see how different and focused the profile becomes:

Job Title: CFO
Industry: Law firm
Head of IT: No
Number of Locations > 1
And the CFO is nervous about compliance and data security.

As a rule of thumb, B-B marketers need more data than B-C marketers. They need information about the companies they are targeting, as well as information about the individuals who are the decision makers and influencers within the companies. B-C marketers have it a bit easier; they just need some demographic information and a little psychographic data, such as interest, fear, or need.

For Can-Do Ideas, we have a fairly straightforward target market: entrepreneurs and marketers who want to grow their brand utilizing content marketing. Most often, they have an established marketing list of at least 1,000 emails or more, and have some complexity in their sales process. They also have to be open to working with an agency.

Through experience, I have learned that if a company doesn't meet one of these criteria, they are probably not a good fit for our services. In our early days, we took on clients who didn't fit the profile, and in almost every case, it came back to haunt us. The last bit about them being open to working with an agency on a long-term basis took some thought.

We realized that small, short-term projects were not something we wanted to pursue. Short-term projects made it hard for us to plan to hire and balance our workloads. Onboarding a new client is expensive, and many companies don't want to pay for the discovery onboarding invariably requires.

There is a hidden pitfall in collecting data about your target audience. The more data you have, the more you are tempted to draw too fine of a conclusion from it. Scientists and marketers are constantly on the lookout for patterns in data that help explain the world, but false indicators can become a time sink and are to be avoided.

As an example, we have been a HubSpot partner for many years, which is a CRM and marketing automation platform. In the early days of HubSpot's partner program, many partners were chasing a profile that HubSpot lovingly called "Marketing Mary."

Mary was described as an early-to-midcareer marketer, who

needs some help managing all her marketing tasks. Many partners rushed to create content for Mary. But there was a big issue. There wasn't enough information about Mary from which to draw insight. What were Mary's pain points? Interests? What were the problems that would drive her to seek a solution? Her problems varied widely among industries and company size, and creating random pieces of content for her imagined issues was not productive.

HOW TO COLLECT DATA

The first source of data is located right in your own company—your sales team. Salespeople are naturally gathering marketing information while meeting with and talking to prospects. Everything that is being said and what is not being said can be valuable for the marketing team to understand more about its personas. Very often, prospects will tell you what their problems are and what they are looking for in a solution. Over a few drinks, they will also talk about their hopes, dreams, and even some of their fears about work and life. Every piece of information is a small glimmer of insight into the complexity of their minds.

One of the largest IT companies in the country once hired me to help them boost sales of a new business unit that was floundering. They had poured resources into the New York market, and their marketing team generated plenty of leads, but the sales team closed very few sales, and both teams were baffled. They had put together an incredible team of seasoned engineers with enormous resources who could provide state-of-the-art IT support. The service just wasn't selling even though many smaller competitors were thriving. So, I listened in on some calls and tagged along with their sales team on appointments; the problem was immediately apparent.

Their sales team was used to working with enterprise clients— think multibillion-dollar Fortune 1000 companies. And all their collateral talked about their value proposition for enterprise clients. Even their client case studies and testimonials were from these amazing companies. But their new target market was small businesses—companies with fewer than 1,000 employees and most typically fewer than 500. The pain points of a director of IT of a 200-person company is vastly different from the pain points of a CTO or CIO of a large enterprise with 5,000 or more employees.

During one meeting with an IT manager of a company with about 175 employees, the salesperson spent more than ten minutes talking about how their US team and their teams in India were able to work together on engineering tickets to provide 24/7 coverage. He name-dropped some of their biggest clients, and I could see he was really impressed with his own presentation.

Then the IT manager asked two questions that exposed some problems, "How many companies our size have you worked with?" he asked. And "We would rather work with a single point of contact locally rather than someone in India. Can you provide that?"

The sales guy was stumped. He hadn't thought through the idea that to a smaller company, the ability to support enterprises and the offering of a global support team, might not be a strength. And they were not set up to provide "a single point of contact" service. They were used to users calling in tickets and then having a team fulfill ticket requests as available. But the personal touch was important to their target market.

They did not win the deal. A few days later, I followed up with the prospect, and they went with a much smaller, local company that never outsourced work. He said he was much more comfortable with the smaller company, because he thought he would actually get better, more personalized service than if he went with a behemoth focused on the enterprise market.

From what I learned from the meetings, I was able to refocus the team and reshape their language and offering for smaller clients. We learned that smaller companies often wanted a single point of contact to work with at the IT company, and many didn't want to always fill out online tickets. Sometimes they just wanted to quickly call and talk through an issue. It was a revelation and helped us segment the database in a very different way.

We suggest marketing teams begin with interviewing their salespeople and ask questions about the people they are meeting with. Look for commonalities and find out what the FAQs of new prospects by persona are. The questions people ask are very revealing. It helps you understand what is important to them beyond the most obvious, "How much does it cost, and what is the delivery time?"

MICRO SURVEYS

Micro surveys are another tool to help your team learn more about your target personas. We start by conducting a content survey and examining what types of content our client has already published, if any, and then we review their top three to five competitors. From there, we brainstorm likely topics of interest based on what we learned, and then we conduct small surveys on those topics. We write topical ads and based on their responses, we choose likely topics to focus on. We are not trying to get a statistically relevant response rate. We just want to know if a certain topic more likely than not has an interest for the target persona.

As an example, we worked with a large engineering and manufacturing company that was focused on heavy industrial verticals, such as aerospace, defense, and transportation. They wanted to create a content offer that would have interest and value to mechanical engineers who were early in their careers—three to five years out of college. They wanted to establish credibility and brand recognition with engineers early in their career with the idea that a long-term relationship that spans years would be beneficial to both sides.

Our team considered many possibilities and narrowed them down to a handful that we thought would have an appeal to the target personas. We wrote a series of small online ads and asked them to vote on what was most important to them. From the survey, we were able to narrow down the idea that improving creativity in engineers was of interest not just to new engineers but also to their managers. After an enormous amount of research and work, the "Engineers' Guide to Improving Creativity" was born, and to date, thousands of engineers have downloaded it with a great amount of positive feedback.

PURCHASING DATA

Demographic and psychographic data is for sale from large data brokers. They gather massive quantities of data on consumers and businesses from sources, such as new home purchase records, business filings, online directories, and phone surveys. You can purchase the data in the millions.

The difficulty for small businesses who want to use purchased data in their digital marketing efforts is that processing the data to gain useful insights on the individuals is difficult. Often the data is still too vague to be useful and does not include the right email addresses so you can match it with your own list.

For example, let's say, over time, I had 5,000 people opt in to my list, and I wanted to learn more about them. I could take my list to a broker and have them match our email addresses with the data they have gathered in their database. The problem is there are an estimated five billion active email addresses in the world, with many people maintaining two or more emails. Most of the brokers are focused on mailing addresses and direct mail. Email is a separate business. They will rarely have anything about my list, and if they do, the question becomes, "How will I use that information in my digital marketing?"

If you have a very large budget and enough time, you can purchase multiple different kinds of lists, cross-reference them, and create profiles on an individual that includes their physical address, email address, and some available psychographic information. Big companies do it, but before you go down that rabbit hole, you need to weigh the enormous costs, time, and technology required. It is a specialized skillset that is beyond most companies. And the good news is, it is mostly unnecessary.

Let's tell the truth. If you buy a list from a broker and send an email to it, you are a spammer. You are sending an unsolicited email to someone you don't know in hopes that they will give you some attention. It can work, but the positioning is weak. What is their first impression? The click-through rates on these types of emails are very low and have big drawbacks.

People who receive your unsolicited email are much more likely to report your email as spam, which will hurt your deliverability. ISPs are motivated to clamp down on spammers, and they take spam reports seriously. Your subsequent emails may not get through at all.

You could try to use an email marketing service such as Mailchimp, My Emma, or Constant Contact, but they all have rules against emailing people who didn't opt in first. They are trying to protect their IP addresses and will clamp down on companies who are getting large numbers of spam reports. They don't allow emailing purchased lists, and it gets worse.

The General Data Protection Regulation (GDPR), a European data privacy act that went into effect in May 2018, **requires opt-in** before you can send an email. They put into law what marketers already knew deep down: if you send someone a cold email, it is spam, and you shouldn't do it. I have already had the next argument at the top of your mind. If you put an opt-out at the bottom of the email and let people unsubscribe, it is not *really* spam, and it is allowed in the US. Just because something is allowed doesn't mean it is something you should do. The GDPR applies to people living in the European Union, but it is a good practice to follow for marketers everywhere. Don't email people unless they have given you permission first.

The best way to build a marketing list is to create content so valuable that your target market can't help but notice and want to come back for more. Create content that helps solve their problems, educates, entertains, and connects with them on an emotional level. Inspire them to connect with you willingly. Instead of pestering them with annoying emails they couldn't care less about, convince them to invite you into their life like an invited guest.

TO GATE OR NOT TO GATE? THAT IS THE QUESTION

As digital marketers, we are faced with a difficult choice. What content do we give away for free, and what content do we ask our readers to tell us something about themselves before we give it to them? It is a real quandary. If we ask for too much, we lose any chance to follow up with them, but if we don't ask for anything, we have no chance.

The challenge is to produce high-quality, free content that is un-gated and even more valuable gated content. The free content must be of high enough value to bring visitors to your website time and time again. Each visit will build a little more of a relationship with them, and if you do it well, it will begin the process of establishing trust. The more trust you can build on the front end, the more information they will be willing to share with you, and the more likely they will do business with you when they are ready.

Gated content has to be so valuable that they are happy to give you their information and look forward to hearing more from you in the future. The best content, where we ask for something in exchange, we call anchor content. It anchors the prospect to your brand. The best anchor content helps the reader in some significant way. It can come in many forms, such as a how-to guide, a template, or maybe just an inspirational piece that helps improve their day. Whatever form your anchor content takes, it must, above everything else, not be boring. It has to engage with the reader in a way that draws them in and inspires them to consume the entire thing and want more.

FREE CONTENT

Most companies are familiar with blogs. Blogging is just a fancy new name for storytelling on your website, and it can be a powerful tool. The reason most corporate blogs fail is because they write anything anyone would ever want to read, and they violate the number one rule of writing—don't be boring. They use jargon and unnecessarily formal words to write in a "professional" voice, and they avoid writing with emotion like it is the plague. In fact, some companies have rules against writing with emotion. It is a formula for disaster.

INSIGHT

It is possible to strategically build a Tribe from the ground up. It takes planning and a deep understanding of all the primary motivations of the Tribe. By understanding the social dynamics that drive individuals, marketers can focus their efforts on creating tribal customs, language, clothing, and other social indicators that help attract and retain members. Just as "Trekkies" have an entire lexicon of language and phrases all their own, a brand can begin to create its own language and take direct action to promote and spread the word to potential members.

The natural tendency of Tribes is toward growth, and to recognize the reluctance of individuals to depart from a group and lose their social ties. These two ideas can be baked into the marketing of a business. The stronger the ties among members, the longer they will stay in a group, and in many cases, the more money they will spend. Membership-based businesses that grow and nurture members as part of a community of like-minded members will outperform businesses that lack a community or that are just transactional in nature.

Opportunities to build social ties among members and the leadership team should be part of the retention and growth strategy. Social ties will help the group maintain cohesion over time, and they will also attract new members who share the core interests and traits of the group. Once you begin to understand the commonalities of a group, you can use them to identify potential new members. There will always be some demographic traits, and they are important, but of much more importance are the psychographic traits of the individuals. What are the internal reasons they want to belong? There may be unconscious reasons for wanting to belong to the group, which are not immediately obvious, and uncovering those reasons is a golden opportunity to build a strong and cohesive group.

One way to help strengthen the socialization within a group is to establish a hierarchy. In most martial arts schools, the hierarchy is established by a recognized belt system, but there are other types of useful hierarchies that can be established. For instance, formalizing leadership positions that are not just voluntary, but are selected is one way.

By elevating a well-deserving member to a leadership position, that person's social tie within the group will strengthen, and many other members will covet the position, the recognition, and tribal standing that comes with it. Many corporations use made-up titles and give lateral promotions to unhappy employees they want to retain. The new positions will often offer identical pay and carry no new duties or responsibilities. They are accepted with open arms, and the new title is worn like a badge of honor. The power of social standing cannot be underestimated.

CAUTION

Overly relying on demographic data and skipping the collection of psychographic data or assuming knowledge of psychographic data is a common mistake. At a minimum, interview a few individuals in your target Tribe. The more authentic your marketing is for your Tribe, the higher chance you will have of connecting with them and of building a relationship. Taking the time to understand the motivations behind a Tribe's behavior is well worth the time and effort.

KEY QUESTIONS

1. How can you increase the socialization of members?
2. What commonalities hold your micro-Tribe together?
3. Is the hierarchy within the group well recognized and prestigious?
4. What specialized language or rituals characterize the Tribe?

CHAPTER THREE

PRIMAL URGES

The first time someone tried to kill me was a surreal experience. It was during the initial invasion of Iraq, and at the time, I was a captain in the Army. I was the commander of an infantry company of more than 300 soldiers in the third battalion of the fifteenth infantry regiment, and I was traveling in my command vehicle (HMMWV, pronounced Humvee). With multiple communication antennae, my vehicle was readily identifiable as an officer's vehicle.

I sat in the passenger seat facing out of the door with my weapon at the ready and a handset attached to my chin strap, so I could communicate with my company and headquarters without turning back toward the front. It was early in the war, and we didn't have the armored HMMWVs they fielded over the next couple of years. I took the doors off the vehicle to improve visibility and to make it easier to return fire from the vehicle. A quick reaction and luck are often needed to survive enemy ambushes.

I was leading a patrol on the outskirts of Baghdad, searching for the body of one of my soldiers. He was killed instantly when he was struck with a rocket-propelled grenade. The explosion blew his body off the top of the truck, and in the confusion of the ensuing battle, he was not immediately recovered. We were on a mission to recover his remains and return them to his wife and five children.

The fifth stanza of the Ranger Creed sums up Army doctrine on recovering lost soldiers. It is something every Ranger understands from the moment they pin on their tab:

"Energetically will I meet the enemies of my country. I shall defeat them on the field of battle, for I am better trained and will fight with all my might. Surrender is not a Ranger word. **I will never leave a fallen comrade to fall into the hands of the enemy** *and under no circumstances will I ever embarrass my country."* The creed is an implied promise. Combat is scary enough without worrying about being left in a foreign country, and I had no intention of leaving him behind.

The intense fighting for control of the main highway into the city had taken its toll. The highway was a chaotic mess of burning vehicles, rubble, and bodies. We were forced to slowly weave our vehicles through the wreckage, and check each body as we went, looking for our missing comrade.

The highway had been cleared of enemy combatants several times, but they kept returning in small units to stage ambushes, and my patrol was caught in one. It's one thing to be in a firefight when the enemy is fifty yards from your position, and you can barely make out individuals, but it is something entirely different when they get up close and personal.

The ambush started with machine-gun fire from two directions and three men rushing our convoy on foot. I found myself looking into the eyes of one of them while he ran at me firing an AK-47. Killing an officer is a significant achievement, and he was doing his best. He was young, barely older than a teenager, with a scraggly black beard and no headgear. It is an odd detail, but I remember wondering how he could run so fast wearing sandals.

For me, it was a surreal couple of moments, and it was my first real lesson in the power of primal urges and emotion. It may sound counterintuitive, but I wasn't scared. I didn't feel even a twinge of fear. It is not that I was brave. I wasn't. Courage requires that you overcome fear, but that is not what I felt at the moment. Instead, I felt an overwhelming urge to react—to stay alive and do something to save myself! It wasn't just a light feeling, like when you feel a bit hungry and are wondering if you should have a piece of pizza or a hamburger. It was the most overpowering surge of adrenaline I had ever felt in my life. I was only thirty-two years old, a newlywed, and when I left for Iraq, my wife was pregnant. I had much to live for.

During the attack, there was no conscious thought or contemplation that took place. My mind and body just reacted and rode the adrenaline like a surfer riding a wave into shore. It clarified my vision and reactions. I had decades of training preparing my actions and reflexes for the moment. I learned to shoot as a kid and I was on the Pistol and Rifle team at West Point, as well as my training as an infantryman.

Luckily for me, the man was running while he fired. I never saw him aim. He just sort of fired in my direction while running.

His bullets hit the front quarter panel of my vehicle, a couple of rounds passed in front of my face and exited the soft top of the vehicle, and a couple of rounds hit the back-right section of the vehicle. He missed me completely.

The last thing you want to do in an ambush is slow down or stop. Your only hope for survival is to fight your way out of the ambush and get out of the kill zone as quickly as possible. I returned fire, and I yelled at my driver to gun it. The entire episode lasted no more than ten to twenty seconds, and then we were charging away.

I am not sure if it was enemy fire or if we ran over something, but our back right tire caught on fire, and we drove all the way to the next allied checkpoint with smoke billowing from our vehicle and praying that our run-flat tire held out and we didn't break down in no man's land. It was a terrible patrol.

Combat is very rarely what you see on TV. It is weeks and months of boredom, interspersed with minutes of terror, rage, and sorrow, and that day was no different. After we got back inside my HQ's security perimeter, and I had a few minutes to process what happened, I realized what a close call it was, and that's when it hit me.

I was completely overcome with emotion—fear, grief, anger, homesickness. My heart raced. My hands shook. It was a few moments of physical and spiritual exhaustion. I was paralyzed. I am sure if I had tried to stand up, I would have passed out. I didn't know it at the time, but it was just the first close call in a long stream of combat missions in Baghdad and later west of Baghdad in a city called Fallujah.

You may be wondering how the lessons of combat helped shape my thinking as a marketer. Most people don't realize it, but one of the primary jobs of an infantry officer during wartime is to manage the emotions of the troops—to fight against the encroachment of negative emotions—and ensure fear, anger, and doubt don't interfere with accomplishing the mission. Soldiers are not robots. They are ruled by their emotions, and as I learned on that hot day in Baghdad, primal urges and emotion are powerful.

My time in the Army gave me unique insight into human nature and another instinct—Tribe. Tribe explains why military units can be so effective together. The military is one of the only places where strangers come together and quickly form a tight-knit bond of trust that transcends normal social barriers. Military units are more than just family units; they are small Tribes. Individuals support and protect one another and risk their very lives for other members of the Tribe.

Tribe also helps explain why peer pressure is so powerful. Teenagers join gangs and experiment with drugs and alcohol at a young age; the Tribe is very prevalent. Our emotions, primal urges, and tribal instincts help to explain much of human behavior. For the last several years, I have studied online content trying to understand why some brand content is productive, or if very well done and with a little luck, goes viral, while other content is ignored. Some brands can scale their businesses through producing blogs, social media posts, white papers, e-books, videos, and podcasts, and other brands are unable to garner any attention for their digital content. I have consulted with large companies with enormous websites that have so little website traffic that if you took down their website, almost no one would notice. In many cases, only one or two pages out of hundreds or even thousands of website pages got any real traffic.

For the longest time the answer eluded me until I started to think about funny kitty videos. They absolutely dominate social media. A Google search for "funny kitty videos" returns 143,000,000 results. The question is: Why? What is the attraction and near-obsession with the cute babies of a different species? The answer can best be explained by anthropology.

Kittens and all baby mammals share certain traits, such as large eyes and soft features, which are genetically encoded to trigger feelings of warmth and protection in adults.[1] A kitten has enough of these traits to trigger many of these feelings in humans. In short, your DNA is coded to make you love kitties. It is a nearly irresistible feeling.

The human impulse to protect the Tribe, especially parents protecting their children, is a fundamental survival mechanism of nearly every species. At birth, human babies are completely helpless. They need many years of constant care in order to survive and thrive. In the wild, especially, human mothers are unable to care for their young, forage for food, and take care of the requirements of shelter and protection alone. The help of others is a vital requirement of survival. This fundamental need is one of the reasons why the Tribe is so important to individuals. Socialization is a survival mechanism left over from our primitive ancestors.

The face of a smiling baby across vastly different cultures evokes similar reactions in individuals. They feel an instant urge to return the smile and have a nearly overwhelming urge to protect the baby. Complete strangers will go out of their way to prevent harm to an infant. It is part of our genetic programming.

Scientists have discovered the protective urge is triggered by the baby's face. The soft doughy skin, big eyes, and diminutive features all evoke the urge. Kitties and puppies share many of the facial traits of a human baby, and they trigger the urge. It helps explain why so many viral posts on Facebook and other social media platforms include babies of all kinds. In fact, the urge is activated by most mammalian young and not just kitties and puppies. Species that do not share those features do evoke the same feelings. Think about the last time you saw a baby spider or cockroach. Chances are, they didn't inspire gushy feelings of love. They don't share the features of a human baby.

An instinct is a genetically coded behavior. All animals have them. Squirrels gather nuts for the winter while geese fly south. Neither has a choice in their behavior. And the same can be said for mating, eating, and many other behaviors in animals. These behaviors are what ensure the survival of a species over the long term.

Humans are different. They have learned to overcome their genetically encoded behaviors. They can decide to fly south for the winter or take a vacation in Hawaii, but free will does not free them from the influence of their original instincts. While they may no longer be considered instincts, they are now what I call "Primal Urges" and exert enormous influence over all behavior.

In the 1940s, Abraham Maslow, an American psychologist,

created what became known as Maslow's hierarchy of needs. It is most often depicted as a five-tier triangle that describes what a human needs to survive, achieve mental health, and ultimately become fulfilled as an individual. There is some controversy among psychologists over the hierarchy, but it serves as a great model to frame the primal urges that help drive human behavior.

"To deny our impulses is to deny what makes us human."
—MOUSE, *THE MATRIX*

Urges are a compulsion to act in some manner, but they are not a certainty. As remnants of human instinct, they draw on the most primal desires of an individual to survive and perpetuate the survival of the species. They influence the acquisition of new knowledge, social cooperation, and individual fulfillment. Urges often defy rational thought, and an individual in the grips of a primal urge will often act in a seemingly irrational manner or exhibit seemingly superhuman traits.

The primal urges that are important for marketers to consider are:

food, clothing, shelter, safety, protection, sex, curiosity, spirituality, and significance

There are other minor urges, such as the need to sleep or the cravings of certain types of addictions, but they do not drive significant human action and are not very useful toward creating brand content that will influence actions within broad groups.

Another view is that all human behavior is based on moving

away from pain and toward pleasure. The idea is useful to keep in mind while developing a marketing campaign, but it is too limited and lacks individual specificity to be helpful when developing a content strategy that will connect with an audience.

A base understanding of the nine major urges described in detail in the next section will help brands create content that connects with their target audiences. If they examine their target Tribes carefully, a large majority of brands will discover a useful urge to keep top of mind while creating great advertisements and content.

At the individual level, the compulsion to act varies within a wide range depending on individual environment, personal experience, and genetic makeup, but in mass, they help explain much of human behavior.

The final three urges are internal to the individual: curiosity, spirituality, and significance. They have nothing to do with survival. Science has not completely explained why humans developed these urges, but every documented human culture has contained some aspect of mass curiosity, divinity, as well as a longing to live a life of meaning that will live on long after our death.

For content creators, the goal is not to try to create an exact measure of what will drive individual behavior. Such a goal is impractical and beyond the scope of science. The goal for marketers is to gain a useful understanding of the urges behind human behavior and incorporate those urges into your sales, marketing, and advertising. Your goal is to increase the influence your content has on your target market to take action.

FOOD

For thousands of years, starvation was one of the main threats to human survival. There was very little food security, and primitive hunter-gatherer tribes spent nearly all their time searching for food. Famine and its accompanying suffering were a constant danger. It limited population growth and helped drive the spread of Homo sapiens across the globe.

In fact, food is such a cornerstone of life, it is one of the few pure instincts preserved in the species. A newborn knows without being taught that to survive, it must suckle, and in the first few days of life outside the womb, newborns devote nearly all their strength and focus on suckling. It is a powerful urge that ensures the survival of the species. Imagine for a moment a child born without the urge. They would quickly weaken and die within days.

Over time, Homo sapiens developed defense mechanisms against starvation. At the onset of hunger, the body reacts by triggering intense cravings for fatty, calorie-dense foods and stomach pains. The mind becomes completely focused on finding sustenance. No other major thoughts can be sustained. Hunger is one of the reasons why children who live in food-insecure homes fall behind in school. When you are hungry, food is all you can think about.

Many years ago, I attended the US Army Ranger school. One of the core tenants of Ranger school is to induce hardship by limiting calories. The instructors purposely starve the students as a test of their mental toughness and to teach them to perform under adverse conditions. Some students become so overwhelmed with the relentless hunger, they can barely function, and many students quit because of it. I personally lost more than thirty pounds during the course and for months afterward, I always carried food with me to help signal to my subconscious mind that I wasn't starving to death.

Like all urges, hunger and the pain it induces can be overcome. The stronger your mind and willpower, the longer you can go without food. Individuals on hunger strikes are able to resist their hunger until they starve themselves to death, but they are a distinct minority. Very few individuals have the willpower or a strong enough reason to do so.

Under the right circumstances, a person can live for a few days without water and three to four weeks without eating, but hunger and thirst will overwhelm an individual's thoughts and actions until food and water are all they can think about. A person who has not eaten or drank anything for just a couple of days will find it very difficult to focus on anything other than satisfying those needs.

Hunger, thirst, and the anti-starvation mentality of the mind are powerful forces in marketing. In the Western world, for the first time in human history, there is an overabundance of calories available to nearly everyone. No one is dying of starvation. Far more pervasive are the ill effects of too many calories—diabetes, high blood pressure, and many other obesity-related illnesses. But calorie riches are a relatively new development for humanity, and we have not adapted in any measurable way. An obese person who goes a couple of days without eating, even though they are in no way in danger of starving to death, will still feel intense hunger pains and cravings just like one of their ancestors who faced real starvation.

The power of food cravings explains why the entire weight-loss industry focuses on the food a person going on a diet can eat versus what cannot be eaten. Look at any weight-loss advertisements from any of the major programs, such as Weight Watchers or Jenny Craig, and you will notice they focus on images of desserts, fried foods, and other culinary delights. They are careful to avoid activating the starvation triggers in viewers, which will discourage them from pursuing weight loss. One of the main reasons losing weight is so difficult is because the body naturally wants to hold calories against times of famine. It is a mental and physical survival adaptation that, although no longer necessary, is still active.

INSIGHT

Cuisine is as personal as clothing or shelter. It is also a unifying tribal trait. Entire micro-Tribes identify themselves around their diets—ketogenic, paleolithic, low carb, vegan, carnivore, gluten-free, low-carb diets, etc. Then there is the enormous variety of styles of cuisines, such as French, Italian, and Chinese.

Sharing a meal with someone has significance in nearly all cultures. It can even have religious overtones such as "Sunday dinner" and "Passover" or a more traditional focus such as in the United States eating turkey on Thanksgiving.

CAUTION

Many of the micro-Tribes around food are polarized online. Ensure you have a deep understanding of the specific group you are developing content for. Otherwise, you will garner the wrong kind of attention. Even small missteps can generate viral vitriol in a very short amount of time. There is no end to controversy around what is considered healthy and environmentally sound food choices, and you must prepare for criticism no matter what you post when it is related to food. For nearly all choices, there is an opposing point of view.

Also, be aware that the emotional connection within these groups is very strong. Science and facts have little bearing on the opinions put forth by groups. Nearly all groups cite dubious studies, blogs, and anecdotal evidence to support their positions. Much of the available information is based on hyperbolic claims by marketers, and there seems to be a deep suspicion of scientists in the field. Ensure you deeply understand a group before developing content for it.

SHELTER

In a wilderness survival situation, finding shelter is almost always the first priority—long before food and even water. Shelter is a human's first line of defense against a harsh world. You can survive for about three days without water and a few weeks without food, but just a few short hours in the cold can spell frostbite, hyperthermia, and death. Humans are not built to resist the elements. They lack the fur, feathers, and thick hides that protect other animals from the elements, and humans use shelter almost like an extension of their frail bodies.

Shelter is a practical human adaptation and has allowed humans to exist in every climate in the world and even in space. It also seems to play a psychological factor because humans will go to great lengths to protect their home, similar to how a bird will attempt to protect its nest. Shelter is the place where people eat, sleep, and socialize with one another. The old saying, "There is no place like home," carries more truth than most people realize.

The home plays an important role in socialization with the Tribe. It is where most people interact with their families on a daily basis, and it is connected to two additional urges we will cover in the next sections—safety and protection. The rules of language and social norms are established and taught in the home, and from an early age, babies are socialized primarily at home until they reach an age where they can venture out on their own.

Shelter is not just for protection from the elements. It provides a haven from dangers of all kinds, including other humans. The home is acknowledged as a safe haven from the world, and a stranger breaking into someone's home is subject to violence, including deadly force. Most laws are lenient when it comes to deadly force used against someone breaking into a home, and homeowners are justified in their use of force to protect themselves inside their homes.

Shelter can also serve as a social signal to the Tribe by acting as a powerful status symbol. In very much the same way clothing showcases an individual's place within the Tribe, a mansion can help establish one's place within the hierarchy of the Tribe. Once it meets the basic needs of shelter and safety, it can then become a social signal to help establish an individual's place in the Tribal hierarchy.

Beyond a place to escape the elements, shelter can also be a major status symbol and social signal. A large and beautiful home is a sign of wealth, prestige, and, very often, power. Celebrities, CEOs, and powerful politicians almost all live in homes that reflect their place in life. Brands that connect the powerful social signaling of shelter with their audiences will be able to communicate with them in a meaningful way.

For decades, the American dream included owning a home in the suburbs with a white picket fence. But social norms are constantly changing. Since the 2008 housing crisis, homeownership is down sharply, and there is a rising trend of bloggers, financial planners, and pundits arguing against the long-held wisdom of homeownership. It is too early to predict where the trend will head, but it is important to be mindful of how it has affected the perceptions of individuals and how they perceive the social signals of a home.

CLOTHING

Clothing provides individual protection against the elements. It takes the place of the fur, hide, or feathers those other animals use to protect themselves from the environment. Based on archaeological evidence, anthropologists posit that early humans clothed themselves almost exclusively in the hides of other animals while they were still living in warm climes.

Evidence of needles and early textiles date back more than 50,000 years and correlate with the migration of Homo sapiens toward colder climes. Improved clothing helped humans adapt to new climates that were wetter and far colder than they previously endured. Clothing made it possible for them to overcome their weaknesses and adapt to completely new environments.

Clothing also plays a social role in human culture. Technology has evolved to create a nearly unlimited variety of colors and styles, and they are used to convey status and help place individuals within micro-Tribes. Clothing is used for social signaling to convey power, wealth, prestige, and many other types of tribal signals as well as perform their usual function of protecting the body against the elements.

A businessman who wears a power suit to the office is sending a signal to the world as much as the teenager dressed in baggy jeans, a hoody, and tattoos. Through their clothes, they are telling the Tribe around them who they are, how they identify with the Tribe, and in some cases, their clothing will determine people's beliefs about how they will act in the world. For example, uniforms send particularly strong social signals. They are widely recognized, and people who observe someone in a uniform will immediately form an image of how that person will probably act, just based on their clothing.

Once the need for warmth and protection are met, the main use of clothing is social signaling. Clothing, especially for women, sends strong signals to the Tribe on an individual's status. Social norms surrounding what types of clothing and how much of the body to cover varies widely among cultures, but wearing clothing beyond their utilitarian use is practiced across nearly all human cultures.

The media is obsessed with clothing. The tabloids are constantly filled with stories about what a celebrity wore (or didn't wear) on the red carpet, how world leaders dress, or even clothing trends of individual groups. From baggy jeans to the latest couture fashion, clothes have something to say about the individual wearing them.

Micro-Tribes will often identify one another through clothing like soldiers on the battlefield identify friend and foe through their uniforms. Two examples are Harley Davidson riders and martial artists who practice Brazilian Jiu-Jitsu. In the 1960s, Harley Davidson riders defined an entire micro-culture around motorcycle apparel. Leather jackets, jeans, bandannas, and a rebel attitude were all meshed to identify the group.

Another example of Tribes identified through their clothing are Brazilian Jiu-Jitsu academies, whose members invariably own several kimonos and garishly colored rash guards. The kimonos and rash guards are often elaborately decorated with cool patches, pictures, and designs. You can always tell a new member of a Jiu-Jitsu academy. They wear T-shirts to class in lieu of rash guards or karate-style kimonos, but after a few months, they almost always conform.

INSIGHT

Like shelter, clothing occupies a place far beyond just utility. Its primary function is social signaling that makes a statement about the wearer. It will often signal membership in a micro-Tribe, even if the wearer is unaware or attempts to deny social signaling. Individuals who deny they have any sense of fashion sensibility are fooling themselves. Ask yourself, why do they dress the way they dress and not in some other manner? There is almost always an underlying social reason.

<table>
<tr><td align="center">CAUTION</td></tr>
</table>

Marketers must have expertise in and be culturally sensitive to the clothing choices of the group they are targeting. It is important to have an insider's perspective. Social norms are very difficult to discern from the outside looking in, and garnering firsthand data is vital.

SAFETY

The urge to live is one of the most powerful human urges. It is literally hardwired into the body. Fear is one of the mechanisms the mind uses to help prepare the body in extreme circumstances to help ensure survival, and it is one of the most important of all urges. It has helped preserve the species by increasing the likelihood of survival during difficult times.

The mind and body's aversion to pain is predicated on safety and self-preservation. When predators were still a major threat to humans, fear was one of the first lines of defense. When the brain perceives a threat, the amygdala activates parts of the motor control system to prepare you to fight, run, or take some action that will help you survive. The distress signal to the body releases adrenaline and other powerful hormones into the bloodstream and helps account for incredible feats of strength and speed exhibited by individuals when they are scared.

Compared to other predators, humans are weak and vulnerable. They lack a thick hide for protection from enemies and the elements, and they have neither fangs nor claws for protection. Their primary means of protection is by banding together with other humans, building shelter, and through the use of tools of all types. Safety in modern humans primarily revolves around protecting themselves from other humans, accidents of all types, and material losses. Society spends an enormous amount of time, resources, and planning to ensure safety. The number of hospitals, police stations, and laws concerning safety is too numerous to name.

The urge for safety is so strong and important that our laws even allow for killing other individuals in self-defense. In most societies throughout history, self-preservation and safety have been considered nearly inviolate, and in modern times, it is recognized as a fundamental human right.

INSIGHT

Linking a brand's content to personal safety is a winning strategy. Who can argue against making the world a safer place? It has been used by many brands to build awareness around new technologies that may differentiate one brand from another. The car industry will often utilize it when new safety technologies are somewhat expensive, and the general population is still becoming aware of them. In recent years, innovations such as side cameras, blind-spot, and collision-detection technologies are all being marketed toward families as additional precautions to avoid the unthinkable and keep loved ones safe.

PROTECTION

Like safety, protection is a concern for the safety of others. People feel fear for others and will go to great lengths to protect them. There is an old cliché that there is nothing more terrifying than a mother trying to protect her cubs. But it is not just mothers.

When my son was born, my wife and I were overjoyed. He was a healthy and cute baby. We didn't know it at the time, but his cuteness would become a vital trait in his long-term well-being. Unfortunately, he developed colic and cried and fussed for weeks on end. Some days he would cry for hours, and there was little my wife or I could do to comfort him. We took him to the doctor multiple times and tried every home remedy we could find. If you have ever been around a baby who is crying for hours on end, you know what a nerve-racking experience it can be for parents, or anyone within hearing distance for that matter.

After weeks of little sleep and mounting frustration, my wife was nearing exhaustion when he finally settled down. He slept quietly for almost an entire night and miraculously woke up happy and smiling. We were sitting on the couch in the living room when my wife said something I never have forgotten.

As she cooed and cuddled our son, she quipped, "Babies are cute because sometimes it is the only thing that keeps them alive."

She was right. The science is very clear. Baby "cuteness" is a survival mechanism.[2]

SCIENTISTS DEFINE AN INSTINCT AS A GENETICALLY CODED BEHAVIOR THAT IS UNALTERABLE.

As an example, mothers protecting their children exhibit an incredibly strong urge, and most mothers will do nearly anything to protect their children. Stories of nearly superhuman feats of strength and courage to protect loved ones are common. The mind and body trigger enormous adrenal responses when danger presents itself, not just to the individual but to those they care about.

Protection primarily revolves around the nuclear family of mothers and fathers, husbands, wives, and children, but also extends to others who are helpless and in need of protection. Firefighters, police, and soldiers routinely put themselves in danger of harm, often for complete strangers. They are able to overcome their own predisposed urge for self-preservation and put the needs of others first. It is a startling example of the powerful urge to protect the Tribe. One hundred and fifty-one Medals of Honor have been awarded to individuals who sacrificed themselves to protect their comrades by jumping on an enemy grenade in order to protect their comrades. They gave their lives to save the lives of others.[3] It is the ultimate sacrifice to give up one's life for others.

Throughout history, self-sacrifice is held as a sacred act. Christianity is based on the idea of God incarnated as a man giving his life to save humanity from sin. But Jesus's sacrifice was not the first of its kind. The story of the Norse god Odin who was hung from the Yggdrasill tree, his side pierced with a spear, has many parallels with Jesus's story, as well as the story of the titan Prometheus who sacrificed himself to give humanity fire. Zeus punished Prometheus by sending an eagle to tear out his liver and eat it in front of his living eyes, only to have it regrow overnight and occur again the next day. Both stories predate the Christian story by thousands of years, and they are not alone. Nearly every culture contains a mythical story of sacrifice. Self-sacrifice is one of the most admirable traits of humankind, and it is often more powerful than self-preservation when it is in the protection of other tribal members, especially of the young or helpless.

INSIGHT

The urge to protect others is a powerful force in marketing. It drives many of the most obvious industries, such as safety equipment, but it also drives some less obvious industries, such as life insurance, home security, law enforcement, and many others. The key factor is to understand that individuals may take some precautions to protect themselves, but they will often go to extreme measures to protect their families.

The security company ADT leverages the primal urge to protect others in their advertising, "When it comes to protecting your loved ones, choose the leader in home security," and they are not alone. Life insurance is almost completely sold by capitalizing on the urge to protect others from the devastating consequences of death. Parents buy it to protect their families from the loss of income in the event of the death of one or more parents. Businesses buy life insurance to protect the livelihoods of the company to protect from the loss of key personnel.

CAUTION

Avoid scare tactics. As the anti-drug and anti-smoking coalitions found out, trying to scare people into doing or not doing something rarely has the intended effect.

SEX

In animals, procreation is one of the most powerful urges. It ensures the survival of the species and the spread of successful and adaptive genes. Human sexuality is much more complicated. It is not just for procreation. It is one of the most pleasurable activities, and humans crave sex. It also plays a powerful role in day-to-day decision-making and is closely intertwined with powerful emotions such as love and lust. Sexual desire is one of the most complex emotions, and while its power varies widely individual to individual, its ability to garner attention cannot be overstated. Sex is one of the dominant thoughts in people's minds. The urban legend that men think about sex every seven seconds has been debunked, but recent surveys indicate that men think about sex on average eighteen times per day and women about half as much,[4] which is significant. Few other desires consume so much human attention.

Sexual desire mixes love and the protective and tribal urges together into a motivational force that is one of the most used techniques of marketers. In just a casual perusal of advertisements targeted toward men, for even everyday items, such as chewing gum, deodorant, and shampoo, sex is used in some form to garner attention. A large majority of them will use overt sexuality or at least a subtle reference to sex in some way. In fact, pornography is one of the most consumed of all media with more than ten pornography sites making the top 300 internet sites in the world with billions of hours of video porn consumed a year.[5]

INSIGHT

The old cliché, "sex sells," is as true now as it was when it was first uttered. There is even a term among marketing professionals to describe its use—cleavage marketing. The term is most often used to describe using sexual images or innuendo to gain attention. It can work even for seemingly unsexy products, such as hamburgers, jeans, cigarettes, and chewing gum. Wherever the imagination can discover naughty thoughts, sex can be used to garner attention. The examples of non-pornographic brands that have used sex to sell are nearly endless.

CAUTION

Brands need to use caution when using sexuality in their content development. There is a hyper-focus on gender issues, and a slight misunderstanding can quickly develop into negative attention. Feminist sensibilities must be a consideration of every campaign that utilizes female sexuality in any way, and it is prudent to get a variety of opinions from both sexes on any campaign before it is widely released.

CURIOSITY

"Look up at the stars and not down at your feet. Try to make sense of what you see and wonder about what makes the universe exist. Be curious."
—STEPHEN HAWKING

The urge to understand not just their local environment, but the entire universe and all of its secrets is a uniquely human trait. Curiosity has arguably driven much of the exploration of the world and the invention of new technologies. The thirst for new knowledge seems to have no limits and drives much human innovation and work. The proverbial expression, "Curiosity killed the cat," is a warning of the potential dangers of losing control of curiosity to obsession and investigating too much.

Curiosity and its place in cognitive function are not well understood by scientists. It is easily detected in both humans and at a low level, in some animals (such as cats) and seems to be related to the development of the brain, especially during early development. But humans and their insatiable curiosity far exceed that displayed by any other species. In fact, curiosity seems to be one of the most defining traits of human beings and, in certain circumstances, can be a nearly overwhelming motivational force.

If you ever doubt the power of curiosity and people's near-obsession with secrets and mysteries, just do a quick search on

Amazon or Netflix using the words "secret" and/or "mystery" of the world or universe. Limiting the search to just books, the word "secret" on Amazon returns more than 90,000 books with the word in the title, and Netflix has an entire library dedicated to various secrets, potential conspiracies, and other curiosity-driving subjects.

Curiosity also helps to explain some pop culture. Each generation questions the world and why things are ordered in the way they are and seeks to find new answers pushing the envelope of what is possible and what is not. They are curious about what they can do with the world, and they want to be different from the previous generation and define the world on their own terms.

INSIGHT

Curiosity is one of the most used urges by marketers. A large portion of headlines is written with the knowledge that by hinting at something interesting or the revelation of a new knowledge or secret will attract more clicks. Clickbait sites almost always employ curiosity-driving headlines mixed with outrageous statements that, if they were true, would be of interest to people.

Legitimate offers can employ curiosity to great effect. By matching the offer to a well-defined Tribe and their known interests, it will increase engagement. And when you deliver actual value and a well-told story that is entertaining, educational, and insightful, it will begin the process of building a relationship with them.

Curiosity is one of the most overused impulses in marketing. It can easily be perceived as clickbait if not paired with valuable and well-prepared content. The difference between a clickbait headline and a well-written headline is value delivery and expectation. (See the section on clickbait to learn more.) Few things can destroy the possibility of building trust than instilling a feeling of being cheated in someone who is viewing your content for the first time.

SIGNIFICANCE

At a certain point in life after the most pressing urges of survival have been solved, the mind starts to think about its place in the universe. It reflects on the great expanse of time since the dawn of history to the present day and realizes what a small part we have played in the great theater of life. It starts to ask the question, "What does it mean?" Does my life have any value, or are we just born, struggle, and die without meaning?

The answer to the question has kept philosophers and religious scholars busy for all of human history. It is the great question that no other creature on Earth ponders. Animals fulfill their role in nature through the programming of their genes. They never have to ask the questions, "Why do I exist?" or "Does my life have meaning?" Living is in and of itself the meaning. Life seeks to perpetuate more life. The entire existence of animals is given to surviving at the individual level and continuing the species. Growth and more life is the point. The struggle and difficulties life demands are the price to pay, but no animal ever pondered if the price is worth the prize.

For Homo sapiens, significance and meaning revolve around relationships within the Tribe and larger issues that are connected to the Tribe's continued existence. Elon Musk's quest to colonize Mars is based on his vision to give mankind a second home. A place that will help ensure the survival of the species if through some catastrophe such as war or a natural event, such as what killed the dinosaurs, strikes. It is a significant vision.

Musk's vision is larger than most, and yet it speaks to the inner urge found in everyone to help the Tribe in some way that will outlast death. Significance can take many forms, most of which do not include grandiose plans to travel to and colonize other planets. A mother's apt attention to her children, and later in life, grandchildren, can become significant to the individual. A father who works hard to support his family despite the drudgery of long, back-breaking hours is another common example of significance. A belief in never doing harm in the world and only perpetuating good is another type of significant contribution.

Regret is one of the most common emotions in the world. In some people, it appears later in life only after they have spent a lifetime struggling for survival and have solved the most pressing issues of food, shelter, safety, and protection. Regret is a powerful emotion, especially when it is linked to answering the question of the significance of an individual's life. Individuals who are dying are filled with regrets that are almost all related to how they lived their lives and the significance of their lives.

Philosophers and religious leaders have wrestled with the significance question and have come up with a variety of answers that have provided comfort to many people. And within the sheer variety of answers is the opportunity for brands. Significance is different for each person. Just as each individual has a unique set of fingerprints and an entirely unique set of genes, what will gain significance in someone's life is highly variable. Their self-confidence, imagination, belief system, and unique life experiences will all influence what they will find significant. The story they assign to every event in their lives will also have a large influence on their outlook on significance.

Brands' stories that connect with the human urge for significance can do well in the marketplace. They help attract attention and develop a following that is focused not just on the value the brand brings to the marketplace but for the cause they support. The success of cause marketing depends greatly on how closely tied the brand is to the cause, the story, and how skillful the brand is at executing across the different social media channels.

What constitutes significance in life varies widely from individual to individual. For most people, it will revolve around a contribution to the greater good of humanity, love, or as a service to their community, family members, and especially children. Support of a good cause, through donations of time, money, or other resources, is another avenue people take to realize feelings of significance. What appeals to one person may have no appeal to others, and it will take some trial and error to understand what is meaningful to a particular group.

INSIGHT

Homo sapiens are at heart a herd animal, and our connections to one another permeate nearly all our drives and the decisions we make on a day-to-day basis. The best marketing identifies these urges and connections and speaks directly to them.

CAUTION

Some individuals equate significance with religion or spirituality. Brands must tread lightly so as not to offend or marginalize any one group. Research to gather data on any group is vital to ensure understanding of what they believe is significant.

SPIRITUALITY

Belief in a sentient force behind all of creation is one of the most pervasive ideas of Homo sapiens. Our ancient ancestors imagined a universe that was ruled by the fickle will of the gods and their belief systems shaped their laws and how they treated one another. Human cultures have always included belief in a spirit world of some sort, and anthropologists have identified more than four thousand religions and five thousand different gods that have played a role in human society throughout history.

Religious belief in the divine continues to help shape human culture. It provides comfort to individuals in an otherwise chaotic and random world, and many of our current political and cultural structures can be traced back to religious roots. It is a powerful force in human behavior, and it is important for brand marketers to be aware of and understand its influence.

Rituals are a major component of religions. They attempt to trigger a sense of connection and sublime wonder with a higher power in the individual. Rituals are one of the major components of religious practice, and many times will be the discerning factor of a religion. For instance, among different sects of the same religion, the beliefs may be similar, but the practice of those beliefs may vary widely.

The feeling of connection with the divine transcends religion, and in nonreligious settings, it most often is connected with nature and a quiet mind. Individuals who spend time alone in nature will often "feel" a connection with a higher power. It is a powerful feeling. Natural beauty, such as soaring mountains, sunrises, sunsets, the ocean, etc., can all evoke feelings of the divine in individuals.

INSIGHT

Incorporating spirituality without the trappings of doctrine or rituals of any individual religion can be a powerful way to connect with a group (unless you are targeting a particular religious group, of course). Spirituality taps into individual longing for a connection with the sublime. Very often, beautiful images, uplifting music, or even prose can evoke spiritual wonder in individuals. Another often-used tactic is to incorporate size disparity by conveying the vastness of the world and even the universe and how we are just a small part of it.

Many brands that are marketing for a destination harness the spiritual urge. They employ beautiful pictures of nature, moving water, and sunshine to convey a back-to-nature feel. They tap into the image of a harried person who just wants to get away from the pace of modern life and get back to their roots of a more serene and spiritual life.

CAUTION

Unless you are trying to reach a specific religious group, ensure focus on spirituality devoid of ritual and doctrine. In a world where hypersensitivity has become the norm, it is easy to offend someone and have even an inadvertent, seemingly innocuous offense grow into a firestorm on social media. Avoid any type of language that could be deemed judgmental or elevating one religion above others.

KEY QUESTIONS

1. What is the most important urge for your Tribe?
2. How does your Tribes' most important urge affect their buying decisions?
3. What is your Tribe afraid of when it comes to your core products or services?

CHAPTER FOUR

PRIMAL EMOTIONS

Emotions are difficult to quantify. Each person experiences feelings in their own unique way, and science does not have an accurate way of measuring emotions other than through self-reporting and yet, they drive much of human behavior.[1] Humans have basic primal urges, such as food, shelter, clothing, and more elevated urges such as curiosity, significance, and spirituality. Primal emotions, on the other hand, can be described as the feelings humans experience and which emerge from these base human drives.

Scientists have determined that most consumer decisions are emotion-based, and logic is used to justify those decisions afterward. The findings have interesting implications for marketers. What if, by building emotion into brand content, you can improve its performance and influence behavior? It turns out, you can, but first, it is helpful to understand a key detail about how emotions are experienced.

In 1972, psychologist Paul Eckman proposed that there are six primary human emotions: happiness, sadness, fear, anger, surprise, and disgust.[2] He based his initial findings on his ability to identify emotions based on the facial expressions of individuals, and he later added embarrassment, excitement, contempt, shame, pride, satisfaction, and amusement.

But facial expressions don't tell the whole story of how someone is feeling. Human emotion is much more complex than can be explained purely through the contraction of groups of facial expressions. People rarely experience emotions in isolation, such as pure fear or anger. Just like I felt a mix of grief, anger, and relief after the ambush, most of the time, individuals feel a mix of emotions in varying gradients.

Emotions are most often felt in groups of two or more or in what researchers from the University of California, Berkley termed as gradients.[3] Gradient emotions are the mix of emotions felt at any one time with varying intensity. For instance, a parent might feel joy, admiration, and relief at the news that their son or daughter is graduating from college with honors. And moments later they feel anxiety and even fear when they contemplate their child venturing out into the world on their own. Susan Krauss Whitbourne, a psychology professor at the University of Massachusetts Amherst, defined emotion as "some combination of arousal plus cognitive interpretation."[4]

The emotions they identified are as follows:

> Admiration, adoration, aesthetic appreciation, amusement, anger, anxiety, awe, awkwardness, boredom, calmness, confusion, craving, curiosity, disgust, empathic pain, entrancement, envy, excitement, fear, horror, isolation, interest, joy, love, loneliness, nostalgia, relief, romance, sadness, satisfaction, sexual desire, and surprise.

Notice that many of the emotions are related to how individuals relate to one another and the world, such as the love a mother feels for her baby, the sorrow a son feels at the passing of his mother, or the anger at a perceived wrong. Thoughts and emotions are closely related and help define an individual's outlook on the world and will eventually determine if they take action or not.

For marketers trying to find the right emotions to focus on for a content marketing program, the following emotions are what I think of as cornerstone emotions. These are some of the most commonly applied emotions by marketers and a quick glance through any large, news-type website will provide multiple examples:

Curiosity, fear, envy, lust, love, excitement, nostalgia, surprise

The most powerful stories leverage both emotion and primal urges. They tap into the essence of what it means to be human and deliver it in a way that connects. Emotion and primal urges, when combined, exert such a powerful hold over individuals that they are understood to sometimes be beyond an individual's ability to control them. And even our laws make allowances for behavior that is influenced by extreme emotion combined with a primal urge.

For example, an otherwise gentle father who kills someone to protect his family; a betrayed lover who kills a rival; a mother stabbing to death a potential rapist; each is treated far differently by the law than if the killings sprung from some other motive, such as theft and robbery. People hear these horrible stories and empathize. There is a near-universal recognition that faced with similar circumstances, we might have the same reaction, because primal emotions and urges are shared among all of humanity.

Any quick review of the academic research into emotions will quickly reveal that psychologists love to split hairs over what emotions are, how many emotions there are, and the degree to which they are experienced by individuals. Some feelings, such as relief, guilt, shame, horror, nostalgia, and awe, are not fully recognized by the scientific community as emotions, but they are still useful to content creators.

The purpose of learning about emotions is not to definitively detail every possible emotion or deeply understand every nuance. What we are trying to do is understand what emotions are generally a driving force into human behavior and use them while crafting stories as a way of not only holding the readers' interest but to connect with them on a human level.

The stories that have stood the test of time tap into primal instincts. They don't just convey information; they connect with readers on an emotional level. They use our shared humanity to say something memorable.

Whether we are aware of them or not, primal emotions are present and prompt us toward action. And we don't naturally have full control over our emotions. Some individuals, through practice and mindfulness, can learn to better control their emotions and reactions, but in unguarded moments, it is extremely difficult.

Human instinct has not been dampened by our technology. We still respond to our primal emotions and the triggers that precede our emotions.

One example of a master, Primal Storyteller, was the radio personality, Paul Harvey. During his long broadcasting career on his segment, *The Rest of the Story*, he told thousands of mini-stories that touched an entire generation of listeners through a mix of emotional appeal and entertaining delivery. He mixed clever storytelling with a unique and interesting speaking style to draw his listeners in and not only educate and inform them, but to entertain them while he did it. He was a mainstay on the radio for decades based on his storytelling ability.

Many of his broadcasts are available online, and if you listen to them, you will immediately recognize his use of primal emotions and urges. He rarely failed to use one or more in a broadcast.

When creating something new, something unique, it is helpful to ask the questions, "How does this emotionally connect with the audience?" and "What emotions will connect with the readers?" "What about this evokes one or more primal emotions and fascination triggers?"

When I was in grade school, my creative writing teacher had a favorite saying for new writers, "Show it. Don't tell it." She was trying to teach us that telling someone a fact is boring and forgettable but if you can show it to them, the telling will be more interesting and memorable. If I could go back, I would add one small change to alter her saying. "Show it *with emotion*. Don't just tell it." Emotion makes all the difference.

CAUTION

In the aftermath of the September 11, 2001, terrorist attacks against the World Trade Center in New York, people around the country developed symptoms of post-traumatic stress syndrome. Individuals with no connections to NYC and who didn't know anyone who died in the attacks watched the videos of the planes hitting the buildings and horrors of the aftermath over and over. The entire event struck a multitude of Primal Storytelling emotions, urges, and Tribe and triggered a worldwide alarm.

Emotion is contagious. It is passing from individual to individual like a virus. Brand storytellers need to tread cautiously when injecting emotion into their messaging. Over-the-top fearmongering can cause people to tune out messages as a defense mechanism. Just like some people turned off their television sets because the trauma was too great to bear in large quantities, they will tune out brand stories.

Environmentalists attempting to sound the alarm about global warming, in their earnest effort to effect change, have fallen into an emotional trap. For decades, climate scientists and well-meaning environmentalists made vastly exaggerated claims about the immediate impacts of global warming. Predictions of global catastrophe, famine, and rising seas flooding coastal cities such as New York City never materialized. Fearmongering backfired and generated enormous skepticism and emotional pushback that is difficult to overcome with logic and science.

"There's a lot of bushwa in our world today. People will spew highfalutin' nonsense like engagement, targeting, re-targeting, and, probably, re-re-re-re-targeting. They'll show you heatmaps that

track eyeballs. *They'll call any blurt, any piece of digital flotsam, content. Other people will tell you that 'no one reads anymore.' They'll do everything but one thing: Make something interesting, something smart, something moving, something human. Something true.*

That's what writers do."[5]

—GEORGE TANNENBAUM, AD AGED BLOG

KEY QUESTIONS

1. What gradient of emotions does my Tribe feel when purchasing?
2. What is the main emotion I want the audience to feel?
3. What emotion(s) do our current clients feel when they purchase from us?

CHAPTER FIVE

THE STORYTELLERS

Imagine our ancestors in ancient times sitting around a fire built at the mouth of a large cave. The fire burns big and bright and pushes back the darkness. The world is a place of mystery and monsters. Every tooth and claw were turned against them. They were weak and slow. Their own skin wasn't even enough to help them survive the elements. Their only protection was each other. Their strength was their Tribe. Their instinct, from the day they were born, was to cling together for protection, help, and love. Together they hunted, killed, and gathered all they needed to survive. Together they drove away the wolves howling in the distance. They faced the merciless weather and cared for one another when someone was hurt or sick. Being alone in the world was a death sentence. No one could survive alone for long. The Tribe was the key to survival. The need for one another was so ingrained that isolation invited despair and even insanity.

Our ancestors' ability to communicate is what allowed them to cooperate in large groups. They could envision and plan into the future and coordinate the efforts of hundreds, or in modern times hundreds of thousands or even millions of people. No single individual could match the power of a Tribe working together. It made them the most formidable predator on Earth. Together they could do almost anything.

Human communication most likely started with a few sounds and grew over time in complexity, detail, and meaning. It melded with the five senses and helped individuals share the past and plan for the future together. It was a means of conveying information and a source of endless entertainment.

Story evolved as one of the primary means by which humans communicate with one another and a means through which they developed language. It helped individuals retain and recall information and was a vital part of socialization. If your survival depended on your small Tribe, knowing every member of your Tribe and how they related to one another was a vital skill, and stories could help you remember it all. In short, humans are storytellers from birth.

Many of the most popular stories in modern times are incredibly ancient. *Little Red Riding Hood*, *Rumpelstiltskin*, and *Beauty and the Beast* can be traced back more than 2,500 years and may very well have existed far longer in purely oral form.[1] Stories reach back to our most ancient beginnings and touch on the emotion, hopes, and dreams of our ancestors. Even after a millennium, they still speak to us. They reach through the years, passing on the ancient wisdom of the world across languages and cultures. Sometimes the stories will change in detail while maintaining their structure and meaning. Dr. Jamie Tehrani identified more than eighty-five variations of *Little Red Riding Hood* across dozens of cultures. The details of the stories varied, but their structural elements were preserved.[2] *Little Red Riding Hood* is a story that touches on the essence of what every parent wants for their child—safety, and it is a fine example of an easy-to-remember story that contains information every parent wants their child to not only remember but to understand and put into practice.

Stories fulfill many roles in society. They convey knowledge and wisdom and, if done well, entertain at the same time. They also play a role in how parents teach their children language and the social norms of the Tribe. Hidden within each story is an intrinsic view of the world. In Western culture, some common views often portrayed in stories are the ideas of individuality, good overcoming evil, and the overarching optimism of the world. In some collectivist Eastern cultures, stories will often focus on the collective good, the importance of contributing to society, and minimizing the importance of individual contributions.

Ancient cave drawings telling the stories of the hunt and fairy tales warning against the dangers of the forest give us a glimpse into how our ancestors thought about their world. They also help us understand the part story played in their lives. Stories were informative, educational, and entertaining as I mentioned before; they were also one of the primary ways people socialized with one another. Through stories, individuals of the Tribe could connect and empathize with one another on a different level and help cement the deep relationships that everyone's survival depended upon.

THE BRAIN REMEMBERS STORIES

Humans are hardwired to remember stories. The brain recalls information using images and organizes associative neurons to activate additional neurons that recall an episode of memory.[3] This helps explain why stories with vivid imagery are so easy to remember.

Modern memory athletes provide a great example of the power of imagery and story in recalling information. Most memory athletes employ a methodology of memorization called **Loci**. The term Loci derives from the Latin word for place, but its more modern meaning as a memory technique derives from the story of the Ancient Greek poet Simonides.[4] As the story goes, Simonides attended a banquet where all the guests sat around a large table. Simonides left the table to greet guests at the door, and while he was gone, the roof of the building collapsed, killing all the guests. It was a terrible accident, and many of the bodies of the dead were badly damaged and unrecognizable.

Simonides employed a memory technique that later became known as the Loci method of memorization. He identified all the guests at the banquet by recalling the place where they sat at the table and linking the place with the individual. His familiarity with the physical makeup of the hall gave his mind a place to store all the information and was the thread that linked all of Simonides's memories together to help him recall the names of everyone who was in the hall.

The Loci methodology relies on memorizing a "memory palace," which is just a place, such as the rooms or objects in a house or the places on a long walk and then putting whatever is being memorized in each of the places. The idea is that the images of what is put in each place must be vivid and unique. It is helpful for each unique object to incorporate sound, movement, color, and micro-stories to make the images unique.

In modern times, stories are the primary way we entertain ourselves, and they are one of the primary ways through which we interact with others. Think about the last time you went to a party. How many stories were being told around you? People talking about their lives, what happened to them, and how? Stories help them bond together through shared experiences, interests, and common values. They help people connect on a deeper level than just a casual acquaintance.

The media is dominated by stories in every form. Movies, television, radio, video games, blogs, and print media of all kinds use stories as the primary means to connect with their target audiences. Very little is published in any form that doesn't attempt to tell a story, and nearly all of the most consumed content is story-based.

Stories work so well because, like the objects placed in the memory palaces, it evokes vivid images within the mind. Long before Simonides's first example of Loci, humans were thinking in images. Modern humans are not very different from their ancestors. From an evolutionary perspective, humans have not been around long enough to adapt to changes in technology that happened in just the last one hundred years or so. They are still driven by the same primal urges today that drove them in 70,000 BC. It is an important understanding that will help content creators create more effective content by speaking to the primal urges and emotions of people. The better that modern marketers understand how stories tap into the primal emotions and impulses of human beings, the more likely they will be able to craft stories that inspire action.

Another argument for the primal nature of storytelling is its ubiquitous presence across cultures. A cursory review of cultures throughout history reveals some important commonalities. Nearly every culture independently developed religion, cuisine, music, language, a social structure, and stories. Stories are one of the great commonalities of history. There is no example of human culture, either living or dead, that did not employ storytelling as a communication tool.

Story, as it pertains to marketing, is not about creating fairy tales as your mother read you when you were little. Story in this context is any content produced on behalf of a brand for a target audience. It is also a reminder that brand content is not just about conveying information. Story is the most powerful tool in the marketing tool kit, and if skillfully done, it has the power to connect, build trust, and begin a relationship with target audiences. Story has always played a fundamental role in human communication, and it remains the number one way marketers grow their brands.

Brand content is fundamentally different from fiction. Its purpose is to increase commerce and to sell more goods or services. Brand content channels Adam Smith as it attempts to match supply with demand and, if successful, increase sales.

To be successful, content creators must recognize a fundamental truism; they are selling to human beings and must contend with the urges, emotions, and social constructs that come with humanity. Even B-B marketers are still selling to people and not to other companies. Remember that companies don't make decisions. Individuals within those companies make decisions and keeping them top of mind when creating content is vital to success. I bring this point up again because forgetting they are marketing to humans is one of the most common mistakes I have found when auditing B-B brand marketing.

Understanding human nature and why we tend to think, feel, and take action on one idea and not another is a great advantage when creating content. Most marketers create content with little thought to the psychological makeup of their target audience. It is almost as if they are writing with the blind hope that their content will accomplish its goals. By applying the *Primal Storytelling* methodology, creators will decrease the time it takes to create good content and improve their results.

More than thirty years ago, social psychologist Robert Cialdini published his book, *Influence, the Psychology of Persuasion.*[5] Since its publication, it has become a classic found on the shelf of nearly every serious marketer. Dr. Cialdini explored six categories of psychological principles that marketers, advertisers, and salespeople use to influence people to buy something. He details and explores six principles—consistency, reciprocity, social proof, authority, liking, and scarcity. Each of his principles is strong and fits perfectly within the primal framework. As you develop your story framework, it can be helpful to review Cialdini's work and integrate his six principles into your own stories.

STORIES SHAPE CULTURE

As we already covered, stories are easy for the brain to remember, and we naturally love to hear and tell them. It doesn't even matter if the stories are true or not. They are so powerful that the power of the ideas they convey can shape and change a culture and entire societies.

Take the war on drugs, for example. Much of the war on drugs was driven by misinformation by powerful stores. In an interview with Tim Ferriss, published in March 2019, *New York Times* bestselling author Michael Pollan described the "moral panic" of the 1960s that turned national sentiment against research into psychedelic drugs. At the time, scientists were studying the drugs and their efficacy in treating a number of ailments, such as cancer pain, psychosis, and depression. The research, in many instances, was promising. The drugs seemed to have valuable and safe use.[6] Research progressed until about 1965 when a series of stories appeared in national media purporting the dangers of the drugs. One particularly disturbing story that gained national attention was the story of a man who, while on LSD, stared into the sun until he went blind. The story electrified the country. It was repeated and cited as fact many times in the media and by "experts." But there was absolutely no truth to the story. It was complete fiction, nothing more than an urban legend.

Although discredited, the story and many other stories of the same vein turned public opinion against drugs in general and psychedelic drugs in particular. The stories were pure propaganda and similar in structure and distribution as the film *Reefer Madness* from the 1930s that was used to stir up public hysteria against marijuana.

The drugs didn't change. They were no more dangerous than when they were first introduced into the market as safe. What changed was the stories people told themselves about the drugs. Even when the stories were known to be untrue, they persisted as urban legends, in some cases, for decades. The stories drove public sentiment against psychedelics, which resulted in them being declared illegal for personal use. This made it nearly impossible for real academic research into psychedelics and marijuana to continue.

In the last few years, medical marijuana has been legalized in more than thirty states and is on track to become legalized at the federal level. It has paved the way for renewed academic research into psychedelic drugs and even further research into marijuana as a means for managing long-term pain and treating certain types of anxiety.

Psychedelics are following a similar path as marijuana. As the stories of the 1960s are debunked, and new stories replace them, they are again gaining acceptance, and academics are incorporating them into their research. They currently show promise in treating a number of mental illnesses, including depression and various forms of trauma, such as PTSD. Institutions such as John Hopkins, no longer hampered by false narratives, are now able to conduct real research into the viability of the drugs. If successful, they will be able to introduce promising new treatments that alleviate suffering for thousands of veterans and others troubled by traumatic experiences.

Another example of stories shaping the national narrative can be found with Mixed Martial arts (MMA). MMA has had similar struggles with stories shaping the culture of what is acceptable and unacceptable. It has followed an almost identical trajectory as psychedelics and marijuana but in a much shorter timeline.

MMA is an unarmed combat competition that draws on ancient roots dating all the way back to 646 BC when Pankration was introduced into the ancient Olympic Games held every four years in Greece. In the original Pankration games, there were only two rules—no biting and no eye-gouging. Competitions lasted until a contestant submitted, was rendered unconscious or died, and in a very limited number of cases, the referee could declare the competition a draw. It was a brutal sport that reflected the near-constant state of warfare on the Greek peninsula and the populace's view that war was a necessary part of civilization.

Despite the ancient roots, when MMA was reintroduced to the world in November 1993, it was not widely embraced. Rorian Gracie, a martial artist from Brazil, wanted to stage a competition to showcase that Brazilian Jiu-Jitsu was the greatest fighting art in the world. He had immigrated to the United States and was trying to promote his martial arts school. He came up with the idea of staging a fighting competition drawing on the ancient Pankration rules and billed it as the Ultimate Fighting Competition (UFC). His idea was to pit martial artists from various disciplines against each other in a contest to showcase which art was superior.

He chose his younger brother Royce Gracie to represent Brazilian Jiu-Jitsu in the competition. Royce was a strategic choice for Rorian. Royce was young and skinny and didn't look like a fighter. Nearly anyone who saw Royce and didn't understand his training and mental toughness underestimated him. He was not what most people imagined as a dangerous fighter, and the world was shocked when Royce defeated all comers, including fighters who were far larger, stronger, and fiercer-looking.

The first few UFCs were successful, but the narrative that grew up around the UFC nearly destroyed it. It began to be seen as a modern-day gladiatorial competition that was brutal and barbaric. The number of horror stories around the sport, mostly unfounded, grew to such a frenzy that in 1996 John McCain, the former senator from Arizona, termed mixed martial arts competitions "human cockfighting" and vowed to do everything he could to outlaw the sport.[7]

Stories of the brutal nature of the fights sprouted urban legends across the country. The most common type of story was that fighters were being maimed and even killed in "Fight Club" style fights in back alleyways and basements. Many states moved to ban mixed martial arts, and politicians from both parties almost unanimously condemned the fights to "protect fighters" and to prevent the spread of the "sport."

The problem was almost none of the stories were true. There hasn't been a death or a life-threatening injury incurred during a fight since the sport was introduced. In fact, there is solid evidence that the sport is far safer than either boxing or football. Boxing and football, until recently, allowed athletes to continue to compete even after they suffered head injuries or had been partially knocked out. Multiple concussions resulting from both football and boxing have been shown to cause traumatic brain injuries in athletes, which MMA has avoided because of the ruleset—once a fighter cannot defend themselves, or cannot continue, the fight is stopped.

It wasn't until Luffa purchased the UFC in 1991 and formalized rulesets that the narrative started to change. Dana White, the president of the UFC, was a former boxer, and he understood the concerns of governing bodies over the safety of the athletes. He took many steps to ease the fears of legislators that the athletes were safe and in no danger of long-term harm.

White introduced a few more rules into modern competitions than there were in ancient times, but the basic premise remains the same. Combatants fight until someone submits, is rendered unconscious, or is deemed unable to defend themselves. Punching, kicking, elbow strikes, armlocks, leg locks, and chokes are all allowed. Additionally, athletes are subject to pre-fight physicals by medical professionals, and strict weight classes are enforced to ensure fighters are fairly equal in size and power. The limits were instituted to help protect fighters from the remote possibility of serious injury or death, but mainly the rules were enacted to change the national narrative. Certain types of strikes that were deemed as too dangerous, such as strikes to the back of the head and gouging the groin, were also prohibited.

Interestingly enough, there were not many more injuries before the new rules, and no deaths. All that matters is the change in perception and the story that the fighters are safer. MMA has been billed by White, a former boxer, as being safer than boxing, and that perception has helped shape the entire sport and made it easier for groups to lobby local lawmakers to legalize the sport.

White's efforts were rewarded. The UFC grew from a small venue into a global brand, and in 2016, it was sold for four billion dollars. The UFC continues to grow and thrive, and its story is becoming more mainstream as people learn more about the fighters and the technical aspects of the sport. Today, MMA is one of the fastest-growing sports in the world and is on its way to worldwide acceptance.

The 2016 presidential election was a landmark year for the power of the story. Social media was inundated with opposing stories from every political leaning, and as was later discovered, many of the stories were patently false. "Fake news," became an international debate and accusations of election manipulation by foreign governments, and propaganda by nearly every political party were hotly debated. Emotional stories dominated the national agenda and deeply divided the country. There is not a way to definitively calculate the effect on the election of the stories for and against each candidate, but we know without a doubt that millions of people consumed the stories and based on the tens of millions of likes, shares, and comments that they made an impact. What remains to be seen is the growing awareness of the effect of the story on elections. How will the government, local leaders, and individuals protect themselves from false narratives?

For brand marketers, it is important to understand the power of stories and their ability to shape narratives. As we dive deeper into the elements of Primal Storytelling, it will become easier for you to recognize the structure of a powerful narrative. By understanding the primal urges, emotions, and tribal tendencies of individuals, marketers can construct stories that help shape online narratives. As we learned in the examples cited, false narratives can be incredibly destructive, and on the flip side of the coin, truthful and positive stories have similar power.

INSIGHT

Story has the power to influence and change perception and culture. If you want to influence behavior in a certain direction, first look at the current narratives around that behavior, and begin to think deeply about how to change the stories people are telling.

CAUTION

Like with the exercise of any type of power, there is a fine line between good intentions and destructive behavior. Avoid trying to manipulate the market with your stories. Manipulation can be effective in the short term, but long term it is a losing strategy.

KEY QUESTIONS

1. What stories does your brand currently tell that defines its place in the market?
2. What is the story your brand would like everyone in your target audience to know?
3. Which of Robert Cialdini's six principles should your brand focus on to tell your story more effectively?

CHAPTER SIX

BRAND STORIES AND THEIR ARCHETYPES

Fictional stories follow recognizable patterns. The patterns give structure to our language and help our minds connect with the characters, imagery, and action. Writers use structures because the familiarity helps the reader understand and anticipate what is happening. Structure is also helpful for brand storytellers. As I mentioned in Chapter 5 for brand storytellers, there are four main story types of brands that connect with their Tribe:

1. Origin stories
2. Vision stories
3. Transformation stories
4. Brand value stories

Each story has a different purpose and slightly different structures, but they all contain the essential elements of a primal story.

ORIGIN STORIES

At West Point, every cadet learns the origin and evolution of warfare. It is the story of how war began at the dawn of history between two local groups who fought with rocks and spears. Over millennia, it evolved into global conflicts fought with space age, autonomous weapons from thousands of miles away. As I went through the course, and later experienced combat firsthand, it was clear to me that the story of war and marketing have similarities. The means of war and marketing change, but the primal urges and emotions behind them remain the same. Innovative new tools are constantly being invented and improved, but humanity itself remains unchanged.

I love superheroes and their origin stories. As a kid, I collected comic books and waited in anticipation every month for the next issue. It was before the big, blockbuster superhero movies, and all I had was my imagination to bring them alive. Like every kid, I always imagined what it would be like to suddenly discover I had a power like invisibility, super strength, or the ability to fly. The origin stories were always the most fascinating. They almost always started when the hero was young like me, and suddenly discovered they were different and "special." They told about the struggle the hero went through coming to grips with being so different in the world and the choice to use their powers for good or for evil.

Brand origin stories follow a similar pattern. What is special about the brand? What is the brand's superpower? How did it come about and why? Does the brand choose to do good? (Very few brands deliberately choose evil.) What is their mission?

VISION STORIES

"I think fundamentally the future is vastly more exciting and interesting if we're a spacefaring civilization and a multi-planet species than if we're not. You want to be inspired by things. You want to wake up in the morning and think the future is going to be great. And that's what being a spacefaring civilization is all about."[1]

—ELON MUSK

SpaceX has a vision like no other—to colonize Mars. The vision alone has drawn in investors and talented employees as well as captured the imagination of the public. Musk's vision for the company, almost by itself, kept the company alive in the early days. It was such a lofty vision that it seemed almost ludicrous. Elon Musk had no background in rocket science, aviation, or engineering, and yet he reimagined space travel and became the leader in a new industry of private space travel.

The vision for your brand doesn't have to be so grandiose as colonizing another planet. But you must have a vision and be able to articulate it in a way that is easy to understand and connects with audiences. It should be an authentic, personalized story. If you just try to pander to the audience and tell them what you think they want to hear, they will see right through it and expose your poor motives.

My vision for *Primal Storytelling* is to help 100,000 businesses improve their marketing through brand storytelling. By improving their marketing, they will grow their businesses, create more jobs, and invest in their communities. By investing in their communities, poverty rates will be reduced. Charitable contributions will lift up those in need. Families will be able to buy homes and provide for their families. It is a harmonic cycle that gathers energy and power as it grows. And it all starts with a story about a vision. I will accomplish this goal through my books, seminars, marketing agency, and through *Primal Storytelling*. I am even building an online academy to help teach *Primal Storytelling* to marketers and entrepreneurs who want to go deep and learn the process. My vision won't happen all at once, but over a long period of time, maybe as long as ten or even twenty years.

TRANSFORMATION STORIES

If you have ever watched a weight loss company advertise by showing the before and after pictures of their customers, you understand transformation stories. Those pictures of seemingly "normal" people who learn how to exercise and eat right and lose hundreds of pounds are truly compelling. We instantly think, "If they can do it, why can't I?" The same idea applies to the customers of most businesses if you think of it as a transformation.

Transformation stories always come in three parts—before, during, and after the transformation.

During the "before" stage, you are highlighting the main character's plight. How was life before they met you? What was their biggest pain point and problem? Why did they suddenly decide to do something about it? What propelled them forward? By asking these questions, you will begin to get to the root of their problem, which will lead to the next stage of the story.

The next stage "during" the transformation is really about their direct experience with your product or service. How did it work? What was good about it? Was the process itself thoughtful, convenient, and helpful? Was it something they could tell others about?

And finally, the results stage. What is their state after having worked with your brand? Did it surpass the expectations and goals (it should!) they had when they first started on their journey? What is the most important thing they accomplished working with you? You don't need to have a physical result you can use in an Instagram picture; it can just be a description of the result. Often, when I work with a company, the tangible results are more followers and social media engagement, but the most important metric is, did they grow sales? Sales are the lifeblood of a business, and if we can improve sales, everything else in the business has the opportunity to improve with the transformation.

Many companies already utilize transformation stories in the form of case studies and even in some long-form customer testimonials, but they have another powerful use case. They can be created as vignettes for the sales team to use during their sales process. The three parts of the transformation can often be boiled down to just a few sentences that fit nicely into a well-honed sales process.

BRAND VALUE STORIES

A brand value story is an underlying idea that links content together over a period of time. Think of an entire season of your favorite show. There is an overarching storyline that ties each episode together, but then each episode is its own mini-adventure. You keep going back to watch the next episode because you want to see "what happens next" to your favorite characters. In the value story, the main character is your customer. They are the real subject, and you want to add value to their life.

There are many examples of long-form value stories, but one of my favorites is one we created for a manufacturing company. This particular company makes precision components and assemblies for many industries, such as medical devices, aerospace, 3D printers, and defense. They have been in business for more than seventy years and have enjoyed great brand awareness during the years with engineers, but over the last few years, they noticed a troubling trend. Many engineers they worked with at their best customers were nearing retirement, and they had few relationships or brand recognition with engineers who had a few years' experience, and they had absolutely no brand recognition with new engineers who were just graduating from college.

They wanted to create a program that could help them connect with a new generation of engineers in a meaningful way. They knew they couldn't just advertise to them because of online noise and they would just be tuned out as part of the tens of thousands of other marketing messages. So, they decided to go in the direction of a value theme. We created a self-improvement and development program for engineers. We produced blogs and white papers around how to improve creativity, leadership, and time management. Then we customized it for an audience of highly educated, left-brained engineers who were already very busy. The program was a great success. Thousands of new engineers engaged with the content, provided positive feedback, and gained brand awareness. It is a long-term campaign, and the path to increased sales is still open, but all the indicators are pointing toward the campaign being a real success.

NONFICTION ARCHETYPES

Works of fiction have many structural elements, but there is one commonality of all stories—they are about a character. The character's world, real or imaginary, is the setting for everything the reader experiences. As the story unfolds, great authors inspire empathy in the audience. They start to root for or against the main character. They will love or hate the character. The emotion they feel is the most important part of the story, far more important than anything that happens. The plot of the story is secondary to their feelings for the character. The purpose of the plot is to reveal more about the nature of the character and to reveal the character's transformation.

Stories fail when they don't inspire a connection with the characters. With every sentence, the author is battling the audience's indifference. The greatest writers create characters the audience can identify with and feel deep empathy for what happens to them. Creating brand stories pose a special challenge—most of them lack central characters and thus do not have a point of view. They tend to provide information in a dry and formal manner and rarely tell stories. Information that is disconnected from a story is harder to remember because it is not easy for the reader to generate images from the content and is less likely to evoke an emotional response. The dilemma becomes how do we tell a nonfiction story from an undefined point of view? Brands must develop characters to give their stories context, plot, and ultimately life.

Lack of narrative voice is one of the reasons companies struggle with stories so much. It is difficult to formulate a story and point of view without a central character to base the story on. Developing a brand character is well worth the effort. There are two main ways to create a brand character—personification and brand representatives.

Personified characters are imaginary characters that give life to the brand story. Geico, McDonald's, Coca-Cola, and thousands of other brands have successfully created imaginary characters that they were able to use to successfully tell their brand stories. They created anthropomorphic characters and imbued them with traits that identified with their target markets (Tribes) and sent them out into the world as the hero of the brand. How many kids in the US don't know about Ronald McDonald or the Coca-Cola bears? And how many adults are unaware of the Geico gecko?

Personification takes enormous creativity and courage by brand leaders to implement. It is such an unusual tactic that it can feel personally risky to the creative team. It is much safer and easier to write another advertisement that is similar to advertisements the brand has used before. How many truck commercials have you seen of a truck driving through rugged terrain with dramatic music playing? Or of a sports car with a bikini model lazing about on its hood? Departments might change agencies or shake up the creative direction, but most advertising is bland, derivative, and barely moves the needle of new sales. The lack of courage in the marketing department is the main reason. Real breakthroughs that can shake up an industry or put a brand on the fast track to exponential growth rarely occur.

The Geico gecko has been a mainstay in Geico's advertising

for more than a decade. His anthropomorphic qualities have endeared him to millions of viewers and helped catapult the brand from the seventh largest auto insurance company in the country to second, just behind Allstate, in 2019. Created by the Martin Agency in Richmond, Virginia, the gecko's endearing human traits, like his quirky accent, help individuals relate to Geico's brand.

Geico is wholly owned by Berkshire Hathaway, whose CEO Warren Buffett has often stated he only buys companies who have a moat around their business. Geico competes in a regulated business. Its products are nearly identical to other insurance companies with only minimal differences. A large part of Geico's "moat" is their advertising, and the gecko and several other personified characters they have showcased over the years, such as the Geico cavemen, are the foundation of their advertising. Personification is a method where the imaginary can manifest itself in the real world and deliver real-world results.

In recent years, technology companies embraced personification by naming and developing quirky personalities into their software programs. Apple's Siri, Amazon's Alexa, and IBM's Watson are three standouts among the many. People naturally assign human traits to the inanimate. From a young age, children name their toys, build complex personalities for them, and tell their stories. It is a part of their process of building context into a world they are learning to understand for the first time. Adults may no longer play with toys as much as when they were children, but they never quite lose the habit of personifying the world. Cherished personal property such as homes and cars are often assigned genders and names, and now that robots are starting to enter the marketplace, the robots are being personified. I experienced this firsthand when my wife brought home a new-generation Roomba, and within a few weeks, he had been painted with a smiley face and outfitted with a name and life story by my children. Socialization is hardwired into the genetic code of individuals, and smart marketers recognize the opportunity.

Personification works because people want to identify with other people—members of the Tribe. It is far easier to relate to an imaginary character, no matter how fanciful, than a meaningless corporate name. People build relationships with people on a one-to-one basis, and by putting a singular face on a large company building, trust is easier. The characters also add context, color, and, if done well, an entertaining element to the brand's stories.

THE REPRESENTATIVE CHARACTER

The second way to create a brand character is through a representative character. The character can be a fictional person played by an actor, such as Dos Equis's "most interesting man in the world," or it can be a real person who assumes the face of the brand. The person assuming the face of the brand doesn't have to be part of the company. They can be an actor or spokesperson, but founders and CEOs who have become the face of the company have also found success connecting with audiences. During the 1980s, Lee Iacocca led the turnaround of Chrysler. A big part of the turnaround was a series of commercials featuring Iacocca. New products introduced at the time certainly helped Chrysler reconnect with the market, but it was Iacocca's charisma, personality, and ability to connect with people that made the big difference. Dave Thomas of Wendy's, Steve Jobs of Apple, and Elon Musk of SpaceX and Tesla are additional examples of celebrity CEOs who tap into the collective yearning of individuals to connect with others. People want to do business with people they like and identify with on a human level. Representative brand characters help build trust. They help individuals envision a brand as a person rather than a big faceless company.

Whether creating a personification of an imaginary character or finding someone to undertake the role as the main character in the brand's story, creating content from a character's point of view is much easier than struggling to create content without a character. Characters help give content a point of view and build context into all the creative in a manner that would be otherwise impossible.

In 1999, Jared Fogle wrote an article describing how he had lost more than 200 pounds by walking every day and limiting his diet to Subway. In 2000, Subway hired Fogle to tell his story. The nationwide reaction to Fogle was overwhelming, and he became the face of the company. After Fogle's very first national campaign, company revenue grew by more than 20 percent, and over the next fifteen years, he helped to add more than nine billion dollars in revenue to the company.[2] Fogle made hundreds of commercials and public appearances for Subway, and his story continued to drive sales until his firing in 2015. After Fogle's departure, Subway sales began a steady year-over-year decline. They faced tough competition and suffered from what is more likely than not over-expansion, but the loss of their pitchman cannot be overestimated.[3] For the first time in nearly a decade, Subway doesn't have a central character to wrap their advertising around, and it shows. There is nothing to separate them from all the other fast-food chains they compete with, especially direct competitors like Jimmy Johns, who makes a similar product. If a person has a choice to eat a generic sandwich or one that is prepared by a company they have some sort of personal identification with, the company with a relationship is going to win every time. The familiarity of the central character makes it feel more comfortable than a faceless corporation.

Fogle was effective as the face of the brand because he was a real person who was easy to relate to and who had a wonderful story. Subway tried more than once to move past him as the core of their marketing, but each time their sales declined, they rehired him. He was a living, breathing testimonial for the company that convinced many people that eating at Subway could be healthier than other choices. Whether or not the healthier choice position was 100 percent correct or not, doesn't matter. Human behavior is irrational, and the tribal connection is much more powerful. What matters is that Fogle was seen as credible and likable, and his endorsement was a sign that Subway was accepted by the "Tribe" and a good choice.

Celebrities who provide endorsements are not brand characters, although they provide social proof and, if well-chosen, increase sales. They only become brand characters if they are retained for the long term. Short campaigns may provide a bump in sales, but they rarely build long-term relationships with audiences. William Shatner and his relationship with Priceline is a good example of a celebrity transcending a mere endorsement and becoming the main character.

ARCHETYPES

Fiction writers have long understood that character archetypes are a useful tool for creating vibrant characters who come alive. Archetypes and their role in stories are fundamental to good storytelling, and Christopher Vogler, in his great work, *The Writer's Journey: Mythic Structures for Writers,* does a masterful job of outlining, defining, and categorizing the major fictional archetypes. The archetypes as he defines them are hero, mentor, threshold guardian, herald, shapeshifter, shadow, ally, and trickster. As he puts it, "There are, of course, many more archetypes as many as there are human qualities to dramatize in stories."

Nonfiction writers have a unique problem. Many of the stories they are creating are information-dense, and the most common story arcs are impractical for nonfiction content. The fictional archetypes have limited usefulness. Nonfiction writers are limited by the structure and purpose of their content. Brand content can have several purposes, such as to inform, educate, or entertain. It may also have a more subtle purpose, such as to build trust, provide context, or segment prospects.

There are five brand archetypes that are useful tools in creating a perspective to help widen the types of content that brand marketers create:

- Mentor
- Ally
- Hero
- Herald
- Royal

Just as Vogler pointed out, there are other archetypes, and

there is a case to be made that in certain situations, they will be helpful. With careful study, you will understand that these five archetypes will cover the large majority of situations, and most of the sub-archetypes you may consider are a subcategory of these. From these five archetypes, you can build a solid foundation of a character and wrap many of your brand stories around them. They will act as a starting place and greatly expand your ability to create content that accomplishes your goals.

Even if your character has not been personified or assumed by someone real, archetypes are still a useful exercise. They fulfill a role in your content that will help provide context for the reader. In fiction, archetypes serve two different functions—psychological and dramatic. The oldest stories from antiquity reflected the collective thinking, both conscious and unconscious, of mankind. Mythical characters are little more than a reflection of the hopes and dreams that spring from the inner place that makes us human. The stories our ancestors told reflected their understanding of the world and their understanding of the psyche of people and their quest to understand the meaning of their lives. From the symbolism of Christlike characters who sacrifice themselves (heroes) for the sake of others, to the mentors and allies who appear in the life of the hero to help him on his journey, archetypes are metaphors of real life. People in our own lives play archetypical roles at some point, and it is not unusual for a person to play more than one role over time. Such as the teacher who assumes the role of a mentor early in life and then later becomes an ally in a job hunt or college admissions process.

For nonfiction content creators, understanding the viewpoint of content is helpful. Think of all the content a brand produces as an ecosystem. Each piece has a relationship and influence on every other piece. Visitors to your ecosystem will experience it in a different way, and planning that experience is an important consideration. Is your intention to assume the role of an ally to your readers? Or are you there to help them solve some difficult problems they are facing or give them a glimpse into the luxurious life of royalty? Your intention and the context of the content matter.

ARCHETYPE AND BRAND CONSISTENCY

The contextual function of the Primal Storytelling archetypes is to give creators an overarching theme around which to build their content ecosystem. Consistency in point of view will help readers understand and identify with your voice. Mixing archetypical points of view can cause confusion in audiences, and the incongruence can lead to a disconnect.

An example of messaging disconnect is often seen with celebrities who have built their entire careers around a carefully crafted image of themselves as royalty. They build their social media channels on hundreds or even thousands of pictures and micro-stories of them jet-setting around the globe while they are sipping champagne and socializing with other celebrities. They announce their affairs and breakups through social media, which are nothing more than the modern-day versions of gossip magazines, as if they are monumental events rather than vacuous attempts at validation and attention.

Then they try to take a stance on a political or social issue, which often triggers ridicule and backlash. Their messaging is incongruent with their archetype. The attempt to shift from royalty to herald or mentor backfires because there is no credibility. In some cases, what makes someone a good royal archetype will disqualify them in the minds of their audience to take on a different role. Releasing a sex tape and a revolving door with rehab will not make it easy to then take on the role of mentor or herald. The audience cannot take them seriously. The celebrity has no credibility or trust on serious issues and by pushing the boundaries of their perceived archetype persona, they risk backlash from their audiences.

Being aware of archetypes and carefully crafting the stories the brand produces while ensuring congruence with that archetype is vital. Familiarity breeds trust, and it doesn't happen in a single instance. Trust requires time and repetition. Archetypical consistency helps brands take a place in the minds of the Tribe they are writing for and makes it easy for them to be remembered in the right way and at the right time.

Consistency and Competition

Consider two rental car companies—Hertz and Budget. They compete in the exact same industry with a near-identical product—transportation. But each has assumed a different archetype and context around their content. Hertz has built its brand around the Royal archetype—premium service, nicer cars, etc. However, Budget's value proposition is in their name and more aligned around the Ally archetype. They are the ally of people taking a trip on a limited budget and who are not expecting real amenities or the "royal" treatment. Neither strategy is right nor wrong but must remain congruent. Imagine if either tried to assume the archetype of the other. For instance, if Budget suddenly increased their prices and introduced a new luxury service featuring rare sports cars and white-glove concierge service, then, more likely than not, the shift would cause confusion and decrease sales. Their "Tribe" doesn't see them as a luxury provider, and Budget would find it difficult to shift their focus.

THE MENTOR

In fiction, the mentor appears as an aide who helps the hero expand their understanding of themselves and the world. The mentor puts the hero on the path of discovering their gifts so they can be successful on their journey. The mentor will often act as a teacher and help the hero develop a new skill or master some new knowledge. Yoda in the *Star Wars* saga mentored a young Luke Skywalker to master the force by first looking inside himself. He helped him realize what all heroes realize—that strength springs from your inner character.

Mentors are always a transitory character. The hero will eventually learn what the mentor has to offer and move on with their journey. In this way, the hero may even surpass the mentor. The mentor will either complete his role in the story and fade from view, or he will transition into the role of ally where he will actively help the hero accomplish their quest, just as Yoda was first mentor and then ally to Luke Skywalker.

Legendary marketer Dan Kennedy built a large following and multiple businesses by positioning himself as a mentor to entrepreneurs and small business owners who wanted to grow their businesses. He published more than a dozen books and hundreds of issues of his "No BS" newsletter and variations of it for decades as a means of connecting with his target audience.

Nearly all of his material focused on skill acquisition in copywriting, marketing, habit formation, mental outlook, etc.

What is even more surprising is that he built his following through face to face meetings before the internet through giving seminars and speeches. He used an interesting model of "self-liquidating" lead generation, where he offered free seminars around the country and gathered phone numbers, addresses, and fax numbers of people who might be interested in his services. He then offered them low-cost items, such as books and newsletters, where someone could learn more and connect with him on a human level.

The books and newsletters were his way of providing value and building trust with his audience. He then used that trust and familiarity to sell high-priced information products, coaching programs, and as he often touted, the highest-priced copywriting service in the country. Most current models have to do with giving away free digital information, but his original model is still valid.

INSIGHT

Choose the mentor archetype when your Tribe is coachable. Teach and coach them into a better life in an authentic and powerful way. The subject matter does not need to be related to your core function in any way. In fact, if it is unrelated to your core, it will be easier for your audience to recognize it as a gift.

Brands positioning themselves as the mentor in their content is a powerful way to connect with an audience who is seeking to improve their skills, habits, or life in some way. The mentor positioning gives the brand a chance to build a relationship with readers and establish expertise early in the relationship by providing enormous value before a paid transaction occurs. Educational brands, such as Udacity and the Code Academy, are obvious candidates for utilizing the mentor archetype, but many other types of companies can don the mantel of mentor through content positioning. A wide variety of industries, such as manufacturers, software providers, financial companies, and service companies can take on the mentor archetype and create content that empowers their audiences with information.

The number one goal of the mentor archetype is to help their audience. Each member of the audience takes on the role of the hero, and they are helped along by their mentor's wisdom and guidance. All the content is focused on teaching, coaching, and mentoring them to master new knowledge that will help them on their individual journey. Their "journey" is a metaphor for their life or career and will present in many forms.

CAUTION

It is important to establish authority and credibility in the areas you plan to provide insight, and the information must be valuable. All the content must be professionally produced and expertly delivered. Poorly done content and positioning can hurt your cause.

As an example, I recently clicked a link to an article on the "entrepreneurial" journey. The article was full of clichés and opinions and devoid of any real insight or valuable facts. It was written by a young woman who was attempting to position herself as a "business coach." She was five years out of college, and her only job experience was working in an appointed position for a local governmental organization. She had never worked in a business, never started a business, nor had she bothered to put in the time and effort to research her audience and learn something they might find valuable. Her presumption of entrepreneurial "expertise" was tenuous at best.

If you are not an expert in a subject, you can either hire one to help create expert content for you, or you can take the time to research, learn, and understand a subject enough to create great content for the target audience, but it takes real work. In today's world, nearly all knowledge is a Google search away. Don't crowd the internet with more fluffy nonsense. It will not help your brand.

THE ALLY

Early Homo sapiens lived in a dangerous world. Predators were a danger, but the real threat was Mother Nature herself. Humans suffer from the extremes of climate—heat, cold, rain, snow, and all the difficulties of the terrain. Survival depended on the cooperation, aid, and protection of others.

A group of cooperating humans is a powerful force that can overcome any predator and is well equipped to survive the elements. If an individual is hurt, the group can provide physical aid, and through specialization, it can provide knowledge and experience far beyond what any single individual can achieve.

When entire societies align, they can accomplish monumental goals or cause the destruction of all life on Earth. They have a nearly unlimited power for good or ill. During the early years of WWII, the allies were losing the war with Germany. France, Belgium, the Netherlands, and Luxembourg were conquered in less than six weeks, and Great Britain's disastrous defeat at Dunkirk nearly ended the war for them. The future looked bleak in 1940. Germany and her allies looked unstoppable. It took Russia attacking from the east, and America, Canada, and many other nations joining the alliance to bring about an end to the war. Millions died in the fighting, and many more millions died from the havoc of the disease and famine that followed.

Societies are also capable of great works. They have created incredible architecture, mass transportation systems, began the exploration of outer space, and built institutions of higher learning and science that continue to improve the lives of humanity. Entire networks of medical providers deliver advanced medicine to billions of people around the world. It is a true miracle of cooperation.

But the most fundamental alliances take place locally at the small community and family level. Communities may come together to accomplish many things that idealistically are for the betterment of the entire community, such as feed the poor, build a new road, or staff a volunteer fire department. At the family level, it is even more basic. Parents work together. They do their best to raise children who grow into productive adults by providing a safe and secure environment. Friends help one another in everyday life.

ALLIES IN BUSINESS AND LITERATURE

Literature reflects the human need for allies—Gandalf, Obi-wan Kenobi, and Dumbledore were all first mentors, and then allies of the heroes in their stories. Allies help the hero overcome all obstacles and defeat their enemies while on their way to their end goal. They may help because they are a friend of the hero, but they may also help out of personal self-interest or some other reason. Regardless of the motivation, the ally's help is invaluable as the hero cannot or does not want to undertake the journey or obstacle on their own. Allies provide resources, knowledge, and assistance as needed. They become advocates of the hero's best interests.

Many service providers will utilize the Ally archetype. For example, financial advisers, CPAs, even lawyers are a natural fit as the Ally archetype. They put the hero's (customer's) best interest first and provide expert help through complex and difficult issues. The hero's life and circumstances are improved by teaming up with someone who expands their capabilities and helps them traverse difficult and complicated situations.

INSIGHT

Brands, such as professional services companies, who position themselves as allies to their customers will win in the long term. Seeking help from allies is a fundamental part of being human, and brands that can help in the most human way possible will form connections their competitors are unable to compete with.

As an example, USAA has positioned itself as the insurance ally to active-duty military, veterans, and their families. They have a near-fanatical customer base, and they built it by creating great affinity with veterans and by providing a service that goes far above and beyond what most people expect from an insurance company. I have used them personally for nearly twenty-five years and would never leave, even if I found a slightly cheaper service.

First, they make doing business with them easy. They have a well-designed online portal that is fast and convenient to use. Second, I once faced a major disaster, and they handled it wonderfully. In 2004, my house was partially destroyed in a storm. A massive tree was pulled out of the ground by its roots and fell down the length of our house. It crushed the carport and roof, damaged my wife's car, and moved the entire house off its foundation. My family was home at the time, and I was very nearly killed in the incident. Needless to say, it was a stressful and difficult time for us both mentally and financially.

In just a few days, they assessed the situation, authorized payments, and helped us find vendors to begin the process of rebuilding. We had to move out of the house, and over the next few months, they were consistently easy to work with and understood what we were going through. They helped us work with professionals and kept track of everything that needed to be done for us to complete the project.

How they distinguished themselves was not in providing insurance. Many companies can provide insurance. It is a commodity. They positioned themselves as a helpful ally who just wanted to help us get our family back into our house as safely and quickly as possible. They were cost-conscious during the project without making it seem like they were trying to be greedy. All in all, it was a seamless experience. I had no complaints with them at all, which was not the experience of thousands of others in our area who had also lost their homes. We heard many insurance company horror stories from friends and people in the community who had the opposite experience we had.

Being perceived as an ally can be a challenge. For instance, banks such as Wells Fargo and Bank of America long positioned themselves as allies to people trying to realize the American dream of owning a home or opening a small business. But in the last twenty years, both banks took a hit to their public perception. Seemingly predatory foreclosures and poor service to individuals and small businesses shook their perception as allies.

The lesson for other brands is, trust is much easier to build and maintain than it is to restore after a perceived betrayal. Neither bank can seriously position themselves as allies of individuals or small businesses. They have squandered much of the public goodwill and trust they spent years building.

THE HERO

Fiction is dominated by stories about heroes and their exploits. They defy the odds with their special gifts to overcome all obstacles and challenges while transforming themselves, hopefully for the better, in the process. Through their journey, they reveal the world at large and their inner world, not just as they are but as they could be. Heroes play a special role within a Tribe—vicarious experience. Everyone wants to be a hero or, at the least, associated with one.

Tribes are hierarchical in nature, and members assume a certain status within the Tribe. Similar to how wolves and apes organize themselves, humans have leaders who serve as the alphas and descending order of social status down to the last member with the least social status. Michael Jordan and Julius Caesar are separated by more than two thousand years of history, and yet they both fulfilled similar roles in society—they were heroes of the people. They were revered by the masses and imbued with near-mythical status despite both being normal human beings. Caesar carefully crafted his image as a hero of the people and often held games and events, such as his triumphant presentation of Cleopatra to the people of Rome, that were engineered to magnify his status as a hero and his place in the hearts and minds of the people.

Brand marketers who carefully craft an image of the hero for their main character can reap the benefits. One such marketer is Richard Branson. From his earliest years as an entrepreneur with Virgin, Branson carefully constructed an image of himself as a dashing heroic figure. He manufactured seemingly impossible quests for himself to accomplish, such as circumventing the globe in a hot-air balloon, that transcended more mundane PR students. On more than one occasion he put himself in real danger for the sake of his public image. His more than 400 companies have benefited enormously from his celebrity status and are purportedly worth more than five billion dollars.

Heroic qualities can be intrinsic to a character like in the case of medal of honor winners and retired generals, such as Norman Schwarzkopf and Colin Powell, or they can be carefully constructed images, such as Elon Musk, who has taken the position as a potential savior of those able to escape Earth to a colony on Mars. Musk plans to colonize Mars in case Earth becomes uninhabitable through war, global warming, or some other world-destroying event, and thus give mankind a fallback habitat to preserve the species. Musk's use of the hero archetype has helped him keep Tesla afloat even though the company has lost money for nearly a decade.

To create a heroic character, you must first determine what qualities of heroism your character possesses. Heroic qualities are not the superpowers a character exhibits in the latest *Marvel* superhero flick. They are the most human qualities amplified by extraordinary results. They most often include an element of personal courage to overcome fear for their own safety, the safety of others, or banishment from the Tribe. Qualities such as courage, compassion, and perseverance in the face of overwhelming odds, danger, or humiliation. The hero is afraid and acts anyway. Or the hero is harmed and yet exhibits anti-fragile qualities, and they grow stronger through adversity.

Nelson Mandela endured decades of imprisonment and political persecution yet emerged seemingly unscathed. Where others in similar circumstances might have left prison bitter, angry, and full of hate for their unjust accusers, he left prison calm and full of a tranquil strength that disarmed his opponents, solidified the support of his allies, and helped overthrow apartheid. He emerged seemingly stronger of mind and spirit than would be expected of someone who experienced such hardship. All of his heroic qualities sprung from his spirit and iron will.

Physical acts of courage such as the soldier who jumps on a grenade; the firefighter who risks her life for a neighbor; or a stranger who renders first aid to someone in a car accident are all easy to see and identify. They are the outward signs of heroic qualities.

In contrast are the inner heroic qualities such as overcoming your inner demons to accomplish something extraordinary; the drug addict who is able to kick their addiction and lead a productive life; the teenage mother who raises her child while pursuing her dream of becoming a doctor; the person with a disability who still accomplishes their dreams.

In every case, heroes accomplish something of significance either physically or mentally. The accomplishment must include great hardship, danger, or personal sacrifice. Something that separates the accomplishment from the mundane world seems as if the character is living in a separate world of their own making.

It is important to be cautious when positioning someone as a hero. Exaggerating or fabricating their story is damaging and should be avoided at all costs. Err on the side of caution and if anything, underplay their most heroic qualities. Let the audience assign them a deeper value on their own through understatement. People hate to be tricked, and falsehoods can only backfire. Betrayal of the Tribe is difficult to overcome and rebuilding trust, although possible, is difficult. The anger and scorn heaped on individuals who falsely claim heroism is tremendous, and the damage of false claims is difficult to repair.

Stolen valor is a relatively new term in the lexicon. It is a term that describes someone who falsely claims military service or awards in order to gain some sort of recognition or advantage. There is a federal law against stolen valor and individuals who have been outed as misrepresenting their service have lost their jobs and been publicly humiliated for their conduct.

In today's connected world, it is nearly impossible to perpetuate a lie long term. False claims may seem like a productive shortcut, but only in the short term. Over time the truth will eventually come to light and there will be a strong penalty to pay. The potential short-term gains are not worth the long-term damage to your reputation.

Donald Miller, the author of *Building a Story Brand*, makes the argument that the client should always be the hero. He is talking about the positioning of your brand in the marketplace, and not the stories you tell about yourself, and how you attract them to you with your content. The hero structure has its place in the marketing kitbag, but it must be used correctly and wisely. As an example, if you have a brain tumor that needs to be removed, do you want the well-renowned brain surgeon who has the highest success rate and is considered a legend in his field, or do you want a new surgeon who has been practicing successfully for a couple of years? It is possible that the newer surgeon is better. Maybe he learned a little known, new procedure that has just been approved, but by the positioning, most people are going to choose the hero surgeon.

Brian Williams's firing is case in point. He fabricated multiple stories that painted himself in a heroic light and he got away with his lies for years until in 2015 his lies caught up to him.[4] In 2015, Williams made comments about some of his reporting on the 2003 invasion of Iraq. His comments were odd and he clearly exaggerated what happened. The slipup caused an enormous amount of public scrutiny of his reporting, and it was found that throughout his career he had exaggerated and lied about his reporting on a regular basis in an attempt to self-aggrandize. The revelation ruined his career.

The most puzzling fact about Williams's fall was that it was unnecessary. He is a talented and charismatic personality. He was successful without the lies and exaggeration. They may have helped his career in the short term, and it is not entirely clear that they did, but the long-term damage to his relationships, career, and reputation were catastrophic.

Another example of a successful "hero" is Jillian Michaels, one of the early trainers from the hit TV show *The Biggest Loser*. Michaels has millions of social media followers, has published bestselling books, and is a sought-after speaker. To some of her followers, she takes on the role of the hero. She is a strong female role model who has made her own choices and risen up from listless teenager to wealthy, successful celebrity. As the hero, her role is to inspire, encourage, and even serve as a role model for other women. Modern culture, especially American culture, celebrates real-life heroes who are able to rise above difficult circumstances in their early lives. Oprah Winfrey, Richard Branson, Anthony Robbins, Michael Jordan, and many other celebrities have embraced the hero role in a way that has helped propel their brands to success.

INSIGHT

Heroes are admired by the world or at least a niche audience. They are a type of celebrity, but they are usually known for something they accomplished rather than for their talent or beautiful looks. To make the hero structure productive, you don't have to aim to be a nationally recognized celebrity who garners attention and status from the entire world. You just have to be a hero to your niche audience, and it can give a brand a large marketing advantage. The hero archetype is a powerful way of garnering attention that transfers to brand success.

CAUTION

Positioning the brand as the hero can backfire. Heroism is perceived in different ways, and some audience members might be turned off by it. The comic book character the Punisher is a great example. *The Punisher* is a long-running Marvel Comics character and Netflix series. If you are unfamiliar with it, the main character, Frank Castle, hunts down criminals who have committed the worst crimes and "punishes" them with death. He is judge, jury, and executioner. But Frank has a code. He is a good man with a good heart and kills only the worst of the worst, doing his best to protect innocent people. The audience is split on whether or not Frank Castle is a hero or if he is just as bad or worse than his victims. It is all in your perspective of Frank Castle.

In many cases, making the client the hero is the right positioning. If they feel overshadowed by the brand's hero positioning, it may repel them. If ever you are in doubt about the potential of the hero structure, choose a different story structure.

THE HERALD

Heralds played a special role in mythology. They were revered as not only the messengers of kings, but as from the gods themselves. The Greek god Hermes was the messenger of the gods and the god of heralds. He presided over the introduction of new knowledge to mankind and it was to him that heralds prayed. When a herald had the difficult job of delivering bad news to a ruler, they prayed to Hermes that their bad news would not result in their execution.

Heralds were also used to precede the king and announce the arrival of the royal party. They later expanded their role and were not only the messengers of the king to the nobility, but they also corresponded with leaders of other nations, and eventually assumed the role of diplomats wielding enormous authority. They were focused on implementing the vision of the king for the future. They became the "heralds" of progress and were one of the ways news about new inventions and events were distributed to the masses.

In literature, heralds often carry important and sometimes dire news and warnings to the hero. Gandalf the Grey in Tolkien's *The Hobbit* started as a mentor to Bilbo Baggins. As Bilbo grew as a hero, Gandalf became his ally, and finally at the end of the book, Gandalf became a herald and delivered the warning of the impending arrival of the great goblin army. Gandalf's warning is vital to the entire plot of the book and the course of the follow-on trilogy, *The Lord of the Rings*. It signified the unity that must exist among elves, dwarves, and men against the great evil of the goblins if they hoped to survive an invasion from Mordor. It was also Bilbo's denouement as a hero. After the battle, he fully recognized the value of peace and living a quiet life among friends and family. His need for adventure was satisfied. His transformation was complete.

The herald as a narrative archetype is often used by startups who are offering something very different to the world. New inventions, new processes, or completely new ways of looking at the world are heralded every day. Often, they will rely on grandiose visions. Thomas Edison was a master at creating grandiose narratives around his inventions to attract investors and to capture the imagination of the public. It was a cornerstone of his business and sustained him throughout his entire career.

Elon Musk is one of the greatest brand storytellers of the twenty-first century, and he has almost exclusively used the herald narrative. His positioning of SpaceX may be the most grandiose vision of modern times, and it is definitely the largest vision of any private company. His vision for SpaceX was to invent from scratch relatively low-cost space travel in order to colonize Mars to ensure the survival of the human species in the event of a cataclysmic event on Earth.[5] Over and over again, his timelines and plans for SpaceX have proven to be overly aggressive, or if you listen to his critics, borderline fiction, but he has built SpaceX into one of the dominant players in the space industry and has secured billions of dollars in contracts. In the early years of SpaceX, Musk's ability to paint an exciting and vivid narrative of colonizing Mars helped him secure investors and capture the imagination of millions. It certainly garnered SpaceX an incredible amount of free PR.

Musk's company Tesla has not fared as well as SpaceX, but he has used the herald narrative in a similar way to drive investment. He has touted Tesla as the company that will make electric, self-driving cars ubiquitous and that they will save millions of lives by reducing the number of accidents and lowering carbon emissions. His predictions for Tesla have been even more fantastic and unreliable than for SpaceX, but arguably the narrative he has built around the company has kept it afloat when it was teetering on the edge of failure. He has focused much of his efforts on helping the public imagine a world where no one needs to drive anymore, human-error related deaths are eliminated, and the total number of deaths in car accidents is reduced by 99 percent. It is an incredible vision. The scientific and engineering reality of his vision is by all accounts years away, but the sheer power of his vision has helped drive enormous interest and investment in the company.

One of the reasons his vision for both companies is so powerful is that he connected his vision to the instinctual urges of survival and protection. It is hard for anyone to argue against wanting to ensure the survival of all of humanity or to save the environment from further degradation. The lofty visions are in perfect alignment with instinctual urges, and he has masterfully weaved plots of rags to riches, the quest, and overcoming the problem into the narrative to keep his audiences interested.

Brands who want to take advantage of the herald archetype must first think deeply about their vision for the future. It must be a lofty and valuable vision that people care about, and the brand must deliver on the vision over time. Elon Musk's vision may have a decades-long timeline, but he has delivered some incredible products on the way to the fulfillment of his vision for both companies. He has endured rockets exploding, faulty batteries in his cars, and many other setbacks, but also incredible videos of giant rockets returning to Earth and landing on tiny platforms, thousands of beautiful electric cars in the marketplace, and self-driving technology that is improving every day.

The vision cannot be an incremental improvement. It must be something extraordinary. If Musk had set his vision on creating a car that got 50 percent more gas mileage or just a reusable rocket, both would have been worthy and valuable goals, but they would not have been big enough ideas to sustain the narrative. Better gas mileage is valuable in a car, but it is not that interesting of a story. It has been done many times before and doesn't connect to one of the impulses in an emotional way.

INSIGHT

Even with an enormous amount of information, the future is always uncertain. The world is a complex and ever-changing place. Generating excitement by painting a vision of a bright future can generate excitement around a new product or service and help ignite a brand's growth. People are altruistic by nature and always interested in how amazing things can be in the future. It is one of the main reasons the word "new" is used so often in advertisements. New is almost always associated with "better," more "innovative," and even often more interesting and exciting.

CAUTION

There is inherent risk in positioning a brand using the herald archetype. The future is fraught with unpredictable events and hidden information. You must proceed cautiously. If the predictions you make are contentious, inaccurate, or something changes in the world and they do not take place, the reaction can be a strong backlash, ridicule, and even accusations of fraud. The night of the 2016 election, Hillary Clinton was all but assured that she would be the nation's next president. She led by a comfortable margin in almost every poll and by all measures, she was the most qualified and experienced candidate. Her opponent was a brash reality television star, who had never been in politics. How could she lose? Hillary Clinton's loss was a stunning turn of events and is an example of how difficult it is to predict the future with any type of certainty.

Al Gore's attempt to position himself as a herald of a pending ecological apocalypse and his book, *The Audacity of Hope*, were a disaster for him. None of his predictions came true and many of his future predictions were debunked. Much of the data he presented in his book was poorly researched and highly political. The book was also disconnected from the realities of science and Gore's personal lifestyle. The disconnect cast even more doubt on his predictions, the veracity of his claims, and he was pilloried in the media. Living in a giant mansion and jet-setting around the world in private jets that were far from environmentally friendly seemed to be too incongruent with the message of his book for people to find him credible.

THE ROYAL

Ancient stories of kings and queens, princes, and the princesses they are trying to save dominate literature. A person's stature within a Tribe determines their noteworthiness and for millennia those of noble birth ruled tribes around the world. Their high place in the Tribe guaranteed their popularity and often came with riches and power. Royalty took on a mythic role. Royalty was idealized by romantic writers of the Middle Ages. It became almost synonymous with chivalry, honor, and even beauty. Writers often wrote about the remarkable beauty, strength, and skill of the nobility, and in many cases, it was more likely than not true. If you were a nearly all-powerful king, why would you settle for anyone less than the most beautiful woman in the land? And what woman could resist the affections of a rich, powerful, and handsome king?

Royalty evokes the imagination, and those of royal birth have always played a special part in storytelling. As early as the eighth century BC, the Greek poet Homer wrote the *Iliad* and the *Odyssey* telling the tale of the Greeks in the Trojan war and the warrior king Odysseus. Odysseus was a hero whose exploits were near godlike. He was one of the world's first superheroes. Through wit, wisdom, and strength of arms, he successfully battled incredible monsters on his way home to his faithful and beautiful wife. Odysseus was the ideal of male masculinity of his time, and his wife the model of beauty, poise, and fidelity. The structure of Homer's stories has been used innumerable times throughout history and still serves as a useful model today, even though our idea of royalty has changed somewhat.

The noble families of the old world were the first celebrities. They were beautiful, rich, and powerful, and their mystique still has power today, but it has changed form. The world of today is still obsessed with celebrity, but they do not have to be of noble birth. They just have to take on the trappings of royalty. They need to project the image of beauty, wealth, and power to their audiences, and if they are successful, very often fame will follow.

Celebrities have become the modern-day nobility, and just like the heroes and heroines of old, they are imbued with traits and status far beyond what is real. The media reports on every detail of their love lives, fashion, successes, and failures. No detail is too small to expound upon. And the attention, whether well-founded or not, is effective. Millions of people a day click on gossip articles about their favorite celebrities. It is big business and sells advertising.

Social media has even given rise to a new type of celebrity—influencers. An influencer is an individual who has built up a significant social media following and has the ability of "influencing" the behavior of their audience. Many social media influencers' goal is to position themselves as royalty, so that their followers can live vicariously through them. They focus on their personal beauty, wealth, and idealized lives and try to project this persona to their audience. If they are successful, they can grow a tremendous Tribe and wield enormous influence and power.

As an archetype, the path to royalty is clear. Create an image that invokes the reader's imagination of the ideal life of a celebrity. The image of you as royalty is more important than the actual truth of your circumstances. You do not need to be rich, beautiful, or talented. You only need the skills necessary to evoke in your audience the illusion that you are. The real skill is in the careful crafting of your public persona.

The royalty archetype is representative of status within a Tribe. The larger and broader the Tribe, the more status will bestow power, wealth, and opportunities. If leveraged intelligently, status can also be a means to finding an attractive mate. There is a reason the king in stories is always married to the most beautiful woman in the land. The same holds true for modern-day celebrities, who are a modern twist on royalty. They often win the most attractive mates.

One example of a brand using the royalty archetype is Kylie

Jenner. At only twenty-one years old, she was able to amass a fortune based on building a giant Instagram and Twitter following. If you peruse her posts, they immediately evoke a sense of exclusive privilege, elegance, and beauty. She was able to leverage the small amount of fame she gained from her role in the reality TV show, *Keeping Up with the Kardashians*, into a real marketing strategy. Her image as a self-appointed princess is her marketing strategy. It doesn't matter who she is as a real person, what she really looks like, or whether or not her physical appearance was medically enhanced or not. The most important factor in her success is that more than 130 million followers on Instagram accept her public persona as something noteworthy. It is not an accident that many of her more than 5,000 pictures depict her in a fantasy princess-type role. She has cast herself in the role and it was convincing to a large audience.

INSIGHT

Celebrity and status are powerful marketing forces. If you can build even a niche celebrity within a small Tribe, such as within an association or industry, the dividends are large. You don't need to be recognizable to the entire world, just to your target audience. If it is not practical to build your own celebrity, then buying a celebrity endorsement can be a powerful tool in the marketing kit bag. And the celebrity doesn't have to be an A-lister. There are local brands that successfully hire well-known individuals in their area to speak for them and they will often produce fantastic results. It is one of the reasons politicians so often seek the endorsement of local officials and local groups. The status and "celebrity" of those groups transfers to them.

CAUTION

Seeking celebrity through anything but authentic means can and will backfire. The inter-webs are full of "wannabe" celebrities posing in front of jets and luxury cars only to be found later to be broke and without any of the trappings of royalty. Another often-outed tactic is to post a picture that is purportedly in some exotic location and then later discovered to be fake. Negative social media attention can move like lightning and is merciless. It can be very difficult to reverse the reputational damage of fake stories. If you are going to seek the spotlight, be as authentic as possible.

KEY QUESTIONS

1. Which of the four brand stories do you think will connect with your audience the fastest?
2. Consider two archetypes that may fit your brand and outline how you could use them with your brand value stories.
3. Which brand character will you choose for your narrative voice?

CHAPTER SEVEN

NONFICTION PLOTS FOR BRANDS

For those who were creative writers or literary buffs in high school or college you might already be familiar with the works of Christopher Booker's *The Seven Basic Plots: Why We Tell Stories*, Joseph Campbell's *Hero with a Thousand Faces*, or Blake Snyder's *Save the Cat! The Last Book on Screenwriting You'll Ever Need*. All three have their own take on various plot lines, how they are structured, and they are used in creating fictional stories, but they don't address nonfiction work, or how brands creating content can utilize plot structures in creating storylines for social media, blogs, corporate videos, etc.

For those not familiar with their work, the big idea is that stories follow basic plots and universal structures. The good news is you don't have to invent anything new! You just need to be aware of the structure of the different plots, and as you are brainstorming imagine how they might apply to the content for your Tribe. The plots will help guide you and give your imagination the structure it needs to do the work of creating remarkable content that connects with your audience.

After an enormous amount of testing, many failures, and some interesting successes, I narrowed down the *Primal Storytelling* system to five basic plots that will work for most brand marketers. They are certainly not all encompassing, but they will work in a large majority of cases.

1. Overcoming the problem
2. The underdog
3. The quest
4. Life's journey
5. Solving the mystery

Each plot type is a guide to help you visualize your upcoming points and the stories you create to connect with your readers. As you watch, listen, and read marketing messages in the coming days, ask yourself, which category do they fit into and how might you use that structure in your own works?

We are not trying to definitively categorize every potential plot structure. We just need a framework from which to work, and a shortcut we can use most of the time to move us from idea to outline to fully formed story, which we can then write and rewrite until it is something useful.

OVERCOMING THE PROBLEM

Whether it is just a minor issue or something huge, it is a story of discovery with a gloriously happy ending that involves your brand helping them achieve their goal of solving their problem.

The story structure follows a very definitive pattern. A character has what they perceive as a problem, and it is an important enough issue to them that they seek out a solution. The solution may not be readily obvious. They may not even be sure there is a solution, but they begin the journey of finding something that will help them overcome the issue. They may not even be able to pinpoint the cause of their issue, and part of the journey will require a process of revelation.

One of the key distinguishing factors of overcoming the problem is the element of pain. It is causing the individual or organization pain. It may be physical or mental pain or just a mere annoyance, but it is causing enough distress that it motivates action toward finding a cure. Nearly every sales training program focuses on the "pain" a prospect is feeling about an issue. They then do their best to position the entire sales process around building trust and value in solving for that issue. People without problems are not generally in the marketplace looking for solutions. This is why so many pharmaceutical companies create commercials and list symptoms people may be experiencing. They are literally trying to convince people they have a problem that needs solving through their drugs.

Everyone has been faced with at least one problem in their lifetime. They need to get a stain out of their jeans; their spouse is cheating on them; they want to scale their marketing; or maybe they just need to lose a little weight. It can be anything that an individual perceives as a problem.

Overcoming the problem is one of the most used plots marketers employ. Companies showcase that they are ready and able to solve their client's most important problems, and then they do a good job at servicing this client, and the referrals from happy customers help attract more customers. It is a harmonic and powerful process.

Brands will often focus on a benefit of the problem-solving service, such as speed, quality, or the fantastic value of the solution. These are added benefits that contribute to the problem-solving process. The market is full of examples from the local auto body repair shop to H&R Block and the Dollar Shave Club.

INSIGHT

Positioning your brand as the solution to the problems of an audience is a tried-and-true structure. It is straightforward, easy to understand, and many brands have used it successfully to build their business. A clear story of how you solve problems can be enough in some situations to catapult your brand to success. The bigger and more painful the problem you can solve, the easier it will be to overcome sales resistance. No one who needed quadruple bypass heart surgery to live asks the surgeon how much it costs. They are completely focused on the one and only question that matters to them—will I live, and if so, for how long?

CAUTION

You can only solve a problem for someone if **they think** they have a problem. The fact that you think they have a problem that needs solving is irrelevant. They must believe it themselves. The "overcoming the problem" story structure most often fails for brands that are trying to convince the market they have a problem that needs solving. There is an old marketing axiom—people buy cures, but not prevention. Getting people to buy something that will prevent a future problem they may have is very difficult and best avoided if possible.

The software as a service industry (SaaS) is full of companies that created products to solve problems that no one cared about, except maybe the founders. Or the problems were so tiny that potential customers were not willing to pay to have them solved. Some problems just don't need to be solved. As an example, how much would you pay to increase the speed of how fast your lights come on when you flip the light switch? $1,000? $100? $0? For most people, the lights come on fast enough.

THE UNDERDOG

America is rich in the folklore of the underdog who overcomes all the odds to win. It is every "rags-to-riches" story ever told. Every little boy and girl know how the story goes—it's the story of Cinderella, Rocky, and Harry Potter. An unlikely hero grows up under extreme adversity. Through determination, hard work, grit, and a little luck, they overcome all obstacles and achieve their dreams. It is one of the most common themes in literature, and it is a winner.

- A young boy challenges a ferocious giant to one-on-one combat and wins—David vs. Goliath.
- A third-rate boxer gets a shot at the championship—Rocky.
- A poor black girl who is sexually abused and beaten as a child becomes a billionaire—Oprah Winfrey.
- A teenage boy dreams of becoming a pilot for the resistance—Luke Skywalker.

- An uneducated farm boy who grows up in abject poverty becomes president—Abe Lincoln.
- A fax machine saleswoman with no business experience starts a company and becomes a billionaire—Sara Blakely.
- A bullied and demeaned orphan boy saves the world from the dark lord—Harry Potter.
- A Jewish girl born during the depression overcomes a lifetime of sexism to become a supreme court justice—Ruth Ginsburg.

Hollywood has produced a never-ending stream of rags-to-riches stories. There is a reason the storyline is so attractive to Hollywood—hope is a powerful belief. It reminds us that anything is possible if we dream big and work hard enough. It uplifts the spirit and whispers, "Why not me?"

Many successful brands like Nike use the rags-to-riches structure in their marketing. Nike showcases athletes from humble beginnings and illustrates how they fight through every physical and mental obstacle to rise to the top of their sport. Their most famous athlete is Michael Jordan. Jordan grew up as one of five children in a lower-middle-class family in North Carolina. He grew up to be arguably the greatest basketball player of all time, winning an unprecedented six NBA championships, five MVP awards, and a gold medal as part of the 1984 US Olympic team.

Off the court, he was also a titanic success. Over the course of his basketball career, he earned ninety-six million dollars, and he was able to leverage his earnings, image, and fame into a net worth of more than two billion dollars. His Jordan Brand Nike shoe line generates more than a billion dollars a year, decades after he retired from the NBA.

A slight twist to the rags-to-riches theme are underdog stories: an unlikely hero battles against a seemingly insurmountable opponent. The opponent is bigger, stronger, and more capable, and the hero somehow wins the day. It's David vs. Goliath; in hockey, 1980's "Miracle on Ice"; in football, 1972's "Immaculate Reception"; in boxing, Buster Douglas vs. Mike Tyson; in politics, Donald Trump vs. Hillary Clinton. The underdog is celebrated in Western culture, and in many cases, an underdog will garner support just because of their status. As you may have noticed, an individual may fit more than one category. Elon Musk, for example, fits Rags to Riches, the Hero, the Royal, and the Herald.

More than 2,800 years ago, the Greek poet Homer wrote two epic poems, the *Iliad*, and the *Odyssey*, and even then, the underdog story was popular. In book seven of the *Iliad*, Homer recounts a story from Nestor's youth when as a young boy, he battled the seemingly invincible giant Ereuthalion. Against the odds, Nestor battled Ereuthalion and won. Nestor's story is nearly identical to the biblical story of David vs. Goliath, and it was likely written more than two hundred years before the first versions of David vs. Goliath.

As the story goes, David was a boy who worked as a shepherd and lived a simple life until the Israelites went to war with the Philistines. Goliath was a giant who was seemingly unbeatable in one-on-one combat. The greatest warriors of Israel's Army were rightfully afraid of the Philistine champion and refused to accept his challenge to fight. David, nevertheless, takes up the challenge.

When Goliath saw David, he was insulted that the Israelites

sent a boy without so much as a sword to fight him. We all know how the story ends. David hits Goliath in the head with a rock and uses Goliath's own sword to cut off Goliath's head.

It is a popular structure that has connected with audiences for thousands of years, and brands have used the story successfully many times. Steve Jobs positioned Apple against Microsoft as the underdog. At the time, Microsoft was the largest computing company in the world, and Jobs intentionally pitted Apple against Microsoft in its advertising.

When he first founded Virgin airlines, Richard Branson positioned Virgin against British Airlines as an underdog with the passion for creating a new kind of airline where service was the top priority. Sara Blakely has often repeated her story of how she founded Spanx. At the time of its founding, she was struggling to make a living selling fax machines and used $5,000 of her own money to start a company. She had never run a company before, had no experience in fashion or clothing design, and still decided to jump into the clothing business.

Another example is Avis Rental car.[1] In 1962, Avis was the number two rental car company in the country.[2] They proudly told the world, "We are number two," and they settled on a slogan that trumpeted their underdog status—"We try harder." They didn't attempt to convince the world that they were better than their rivals. They fully embraced their underdog status and accepted that their competitor was bigger and more popular. Their slogan persisted for fifty years before it was finally replaced in 2012.

The old saying, "Everyone roots for the underdog," is still true today. Rags to riches and underdog stories resonate with audiences. They inspire hope and convey that with passion and determination, anything is possible. Brands that embrace the themes in an authentic way will find they are able to connect with audiences in a powerful way. The underdog theme has particular power in America where hard work and individualism are idealized. Krystal Overmyer, in her article, "The Psychological Appeal of Underdog Brand Positioning," summed it up best by saying, "When underdogs demonstrate their passion, heart, and perseverance against the odds, we can't help but feel moved. Smart brands can utilize these storytelling components to their advantage."[3]

CAUTION

Brand positioning as an underdog must be authentic. Even a hint of hypocrisy can be an incredible turnoff to audiences and can even create backlash. Large, well-established brands must be cautious, trying to embrace their "humble" roots. If not well done, it can seem disingenuous and cause audiences to seek alternatives they can better connect with.

THE QUEST

The quest can sometimes be confused with overcoming the problem or life's journey, but there are key differences. There are problems and a journey along the way to the end of the hero's quest, but they are secondary to the accomplishment of the hero's goal. The accomplishment of the goal is of utmost importance to the hero, and everything in the story is secondary to that goal.

During the journey, adventure ensues, the mysteries of the world are revealed, something valuable is learned, and the hero(es) is (are) transformed into someone new. Often the transformation is the movement from adolescence to adulthood, but it can take on many forms. In some storylines, the transformation becomes nearly as important as the end goal, but in the end, the quest is the most important part of the story, and without it, the entire storyline falls apart.

Problems encountered along the way to the goal help the hero complete her transformation, but again they are secondary to the accomplishment of the quest. Frodo traveled to Mordor to destroy the ring of doom. Luke traveled the universe to become a Jedi in order to destroy the Death Star. Rocky Balboa's journey was the intense training he underwent before he fought Apollo Creed. Each hero underwent a metamorphosis that, in the end, left them a different person altogether. Without the end goal, each of the journeys and the problems encountered would be pointless.

The quest is one of the most recognizable themes in art and literature, and it is used with great success by marketers. Brands in diverse industries such as education, sports, and even politics use it successfully. It is a compelling narrative that if carefully crafted, it can help people imagine themselves taking the journey toward their goal.

Colleges and universities often use the quest as part of their marketing. They paint the picture of their students pursuing higher education as an epic journey with the goal of earning a diploma and winning the treasure of a better life that comes with it.

Brands that market courses, certifications, and other information will also use the quest. They will often focus on the benefits of the transformation gained during the journey and the new life the hero will enjoy after accomplishing their goal. It is very similar to marketing, but usually along a shorter timeline.

The Olympics uses the quest for a gold medal as one of their recurring stories, and they never seem to get old. The Olympics are not just about competing, the beauty of the athletes, or the thrill of the competition. They are about the individual athletes' struggle to overcome all obstacles, and how they transform as people and athletes to ultimately win the gold medal. Every Olympics uses the same story model applied to a fresh group of athletes.

Their stories never get old. How many people were transfixed by the arc of Michael Phelps's story? He started his quest for gold as a young boy who, in his earliest years, didn't show many signs of the talent he would eventually possess. He toiled for years driven only by his love of swimming, giving up what many would consider a "normal" childhood and never missed practice for years. Finally, he wins his first gold medal, and then he defies all expectations and, over the course of a career, becomes the winningest Olympian of all time, amassing twenty-three gold, two silver, and three bronze medals for a total of twenty-eight medals. Everyone loves a winner.

Politicians often craft their stories using the quest model.

Donald Trump's 2016 presidential campaign is a recent and memorable example. Nearly all of his marketing revolved around a carefully constructed plot line that he used during the primaries and the subsequent election. He couched his quest not just to win the presidency for himself, but to "drain the swamp" of career politicians in Washington in order to "Make America Great Again." He stuck to this storyline with little deviation, coming back to it in speech after speech. All his other platform promises were peripheral to this central theme.

And then he did something that every brand can learn a lesson from; he invited people to join him on his quest. He asked for their help and support. It was a simple, clear, and concise storyline that he retold in different ways, over and over again.

INSIGHT

Brands can use the quest in creative ways to connect with audiences. It is a storyline that connects with people and, if well done, can generate attention and connection. Many of life's goals can be structured as a quest. For example, recruiting and job placement companies can use the quest to paint the picture that they are not there to just help someone with a single job but to help them along with their entire career. The brand becomes the mentor in the hero's journey toward their goal of a fulfilling career that brings them stability, happiness, and a comfortable life. Financial planners and other professionals can use the structure to help paint the picture of their clients' epic struggle to achieve financial independence or to have a happy and comfortable retirement. The applications are nearly endless.

LIFE'S JOURNEY

One of the most common metaphors is the idea of life as a journey with no fixed destination in mind. There is only the moment and what is happening now. Like a journey, life contains a beginning, middle, and end. It contains many adventures and accomplishments, and if it is a life well-lived, it will span the emotional spectrum of love, happiness, sadness, and even hate. Destinations along the journey are just waypoints to help add context to cherished memories. The journey is as the journey does.

Life is more than a series of events. It is filled with conflicting emotions, and above all else tells the story of why life is not easy. It is a journey with, hopefully, adventure along the way. It is full of ups and downs, trials, and tribulations. It is at the end of the day, a journey that is worth taking with no ultimate goal. Think of it like the sightseeing trips you took as a kid. You and the family drove and took in the sights just for the pleasure of it. Many storytellers use this plot to invoke feelings of pleasure, nostalgia, and of living a good life with higher aspirations.

Dunkin Donuts has a long-running series, "Hooked on Dunkin." All of their pieces do a good job of linking donuts to living the good life. Whether you believe donuts are good for the world or not, they have done very well. The commercials evoke a feeling of fun and guilty pleasure.

Another good example of life's journey was the Dos Equis's "Most Interesting Man in the World" campaign. They tied their beer into the idea that a well-dressed, debonair gentleman was living an incredible life because he was drinking their beer. It was funny and interesting and spawned a tidal wave of knock-offs and memes across the internet. But most of all, it invoked a deep feeling that life is a journey.

Nike produced one of my all-time favorite commercials using life's journey. (Yes, I know having a favorite commercial is really geeky.) They hired Casey Neistat, a videographer, and he came up with a brilliant piece called *Make it Count*.[4] Casey took the entire budget for the commercial and traveled around the world, hitting thirteen countries in two weeks. In each country, he made a short clip of his time there. He highlighted the joy of his journey. The big clue of why this is life's journey and not one of the other categories is because there is no real conclusion to making it count. It is a series of events with no real point other than the potential for a life well lived.

Lifestyle brands will often incorporate the life's journey plot. They tell vignettes about people who are making memories— swimming in the ocean, climbing mountains, seeing exotic places, etc. Travel destinations such as Aruba and the Bahamas become beacons to a better life. Jack Kerouac's book, *On the Road*, captures the ideal perfectly.

The tragedies of life are put into perspective. Hardship is inevitable, but like all destinations and adventures on a journey, it, too, will pass. Every experience, whether happy or sad, termed good or bad, is temporary, just as all life is temporary. The journey goes ever onward and is in and unto itself the goal.

The happiest times of life become treasured memories. They help give life meaning and are a sign of a life well lived. Marriage, the birth of a child, graduation from college, vacations, and a thousand small moments all come together to comprise the story of life.

INSIGHT

Nearly everyone recognizes the metaphor of a journey with their life. It is a solid theme that can connect with a wide variety of audiences.

CAUTION

As a plot structure, life's journey is so often used by marketers, it is almost a cliché. It is vital to find a brand-specific hook that will create a strong connection with the journey to avoid feeling like you are just jumping on the bandwagon of other content.

SOLVING THE MYSTERY

In 1887, Arthur Conan Doyle published the first Sherlock Holmes story, *A Study in Scarlet*. It was not the first mystery ever published, although, its immense popularity marks it as the beginning of the worldwide phenomenon of mystery as its own genre of fiction. It is a great example of people's fascination with secrets. One of the most used literary techniques is to slowly unfold the answers to a mystery. Build suspense. Create tension and anticipation in the audience.

We still don't know everything about our world. We haven't delved into everything the world has to offer. The world and the universe are still full of mystery. Bigfoot, the Lockness monster, the secrets of Stonehenge, and the question whether aliens have visited Earth are all obvious "mysteries" that hold people's attention, but there are many more subtle mysteries.

Curiosity and the need to understand is a deeply ingrained human need. Marketers use mystery as a key to many themes. One example is the teaser trailers at the end of many of the *Marvel* movies. If you wait until after the credits at the end of the movie have played, they will often add another clip. The trailer is just a glimpse of what's to come. It creates some mystique around what is to come and stirs the curiosity of the viewer, who then has the urge to solve the mystery with the next movie. It is a brilliant stratagem and from all evidence is working brilliantly for Marvel.

Old-time direct marketers were famous for their use of mystery to drive behavior. They often employed cliff-hangers and statements such as, "The Never Before Revealed," and "The One Secret to Success." And you can replace the word "success" in the last line with just about anything, "The One Secret to ___." The phrase evokes a mini-mystery in the mind that many people just cannot resist. Curiosity is a powerful driving force, and even with its overuse in the media, it still drives clicks and traffic.

Just glance at the bottom of any of the large, news websites, and you will see, often, more than one headline for the latest celebrity secret. *Jane's Wedding Secret Revealed! Mary's One Weight Loss Secret, etc.* Even though you know it is some trivial BS thing, you still feel the urge to click, and many people do. It is clickbait for a reason—it works! Or they use a slightly more subtle tactic where they will leave out exactly what they are describing: *These Cars are The Best of 2019. These are the Hottest Bikini Bodies of the Summer!* It is a formula. "These ___ Are the _____" I made these headlines up, but you will recognize the patterns everywhere. The mysteries of the universe are still being revealed one by one.

Solving the mystery can also apply to tangible problems such as solving a reoccurring business problem, technical issue, or other problems an individual or organization is experiencing.

INSIGHT

Curiosity is a powerful driving force in the human psyche, and if used well, it will capture the attention of your audience and help them connect with your brand.

CAUTION

Curiosity and "secrets" are often overhyped. If they are used as clickbait and do not deliver any type of real insight, they can push the audience away. The point of using curiosity is to attract the audience to the brand. It is important to deliver real value.

An outrage-inducing headline may be fine, but the content has to deliver value to match. It is nonnegotiable. You are trying to build a relationship with someone you just met. If you leave them feeling tricked, it will be difficult for them to trust you and believe anything else you say. Imagine being caught in a lie on a first date. How likely is a second date? Not likely at all.

Marketers creating corporate content seem to believe that to be taken seriously and reflect well on the brand, they must be serious and write in a dry, educational manner. Pompous, over-written, and void of human emotion are not the hallmarks of professional writing. They are the signs of a lack of skill. Even the most conservative businessman, sitting in his Madison Avenue office with a view, is a human being and appreciates a well-told story that delivers value.

Can all content deliver emotional impact in story form? No. But a large amount can be wrapped into story form and salted with emotion, primal urges, and tribal language. There is an urban legend that while in a bar, Ernest Hemingway was challenged in a bet that he couldn't compose a story in six words or less.[5] As the story goes, he wrote:

"Baby Shoes
For Sale
Never Used"

The story delivers emotion more by what is not stated. The technique is powerful because it forces the reader's mind to fill in the details.

One powerful example of well-done emotional brand content was the 2013 Super Bowl ad for Ram trucks. In the ad, Ram played a speech by the radio commentator, Paul Harvey, in the background of the video. Harvey's picturesque language and style helped propel the video, as of this writing, to more than twenty-three million views.[6] The video invokes the emotions of nostalgia and happiness as well as touches the primal urges of food, shelter, and safety, and farmers as a Tribe. It hits every element of Primal Storytelling in an engaging way.

Trust begins by delivering value in an authentic, engaging, and human way. By ensuring the absolute congruence between your headlines and content, the audience won't feel deceived, and if well done will reward your content with their attention. Honesty and truthfulness can be disarming and powerful brand builders.

KEY QUESTIONS

1. What plot structures best fit my brand's overall message?
2. Which plot structures might I apply with some creativity?
3. Is the brand currently using a plot structure, even if unknowingly?
4. What other plot structures might I experiment with over the next ninety days?

CHAPTER EIGHT

THE ART OF MARKETING

The one trait shared by all art is authenticity. We value authenticity as one of our highest virtues. Original artwork is always more valuable than reproductions made from the original. The original is authentic, and it holds a truth from the artist. It is not trying to sell something, nor does it want anything from the audience.

Authenticity matters because audiences can sense truth. They can feel your intentions through the words and images you use. And the opposite is also true. They will know when you are trying to trick them. They may not consciously think it, but their instincts will kick in, and your work will repel them on a subconscious level. Shoddy work written to capture someone's information will not build trust and grow your audience. If it doesn't provide some value and insight, your Tribe will recognize it. If the work is selfish, and all about your brand and what you can get from your audience, it will fail over the long term.

If I put my entire self into the work, it shows. Even though my name is not Michelangelo, the love shines through. When you put everything into the work, audiences' instincts kick in, and they sense you care more about helping them than helping yourself. Selfless acts are attractive and activate a type of cosmic karma.

Building trust with a stranger is not easy. Everyone has been betrayed by a friend, taken advantage of, or just flat out ripped off. It hurts and we never want it to happen again, and it explains why people are so cynical about most marketers. Promises are easy, and cheap promises that are easily broken damage our ability to build trust with the next person. You've likely heard, "I will call you" or "I will finish that for you by Friday or next Tuesday" many times.

The care you take with your art will help build trust by itself. It shows that deep down the work matters, and through the work, the audience matters. Sloppy, late, and disheveled work accomplishes the opposite. It shows that the work didn't matter much to you. Everyone knows you could do better, but you were too busy or didn't care enough to put yourself into your work in a way to create something that matters to someone else.

There are no longer just three channels on TV, two types of cola, or just a few types of breakfast cereal. For the first time in human history, people have endless choices, and the number of alternatives people have for your message and product are nearly limitless. Search Engine Optimization (SEO) as a business is a modern-day scam. Companies are trying to convince brands to create content for search engines. They forgot that real people are searching for solutions to their problems. These people want help, but they have been burned by exaggerated or even false promises.

If you want to be heard by your audience, they have to connect with you and trust you. These are the requirements for them to one day choose you to help them with their problems. And even if you create something that connects with them, they are only going to choose you when they are ready. It is not something you can force or artificially hurry. The most valuable commodity is your audience's attention, and they will only give it when they are ready.

The first time you begin to think of marketing like art, two things will happen. First, you will feel a deep sense of fear. Your brain will see all of the risks of such a "crazy" idea and set off your alarm bells. Your heart rate will increase. You might even feel a surge of adrenaline and the need to take deep breaths. Your brain doesn't want to help you create art. It wants to keep you alive. It hasn't had enough time to adapt to the fact that physical danger is 99 percent in the past and perceives all risk as mortal threats. And what could be riskier than bringing art into marketing a business?

Second, your mind will develop a thousand potential excuses of why you shouldn't do it. Our team members are technically sound, but they are not artists. No one cares about art. We are trying to inspire action to make more sales. Artists are all prima donnas. We are businesspeople, and business is serious. The boss/team/customers won't like it. The list of reasons why you shouldn't create art are endless.

Neither the fear nor the reasons keeping you from approaching your work as a marketer and artist are real. They are what Steven Pressfield, in his book *The War of Art*, named the Resistance. The first time I read the book, I was in awe of his ability to describe my life. He is a modern-day fortune-teller, a seer without equal. We never met, and yet he wrote about my exact fear of sitting down to do the work. I am "just" a marketer. Who am I to dare? The resistance is just as real for marketers as it is for any other creative.

Art is about being more human. People want more connection with real people and it is why sometimes efficiency is so off-putting. Auto attendants are the most efficient way for a company to handle a large volume of inbound calls, but everyone hates them. They are a faceless assembly line and you are the widget moving along the conveyor belt. They are so repellent because people don't want to do business with a faceless company. They want to do business with a trusted friend. No one believes the repeated messages, "Your call is important to us. And we are experiencing higher call volumes than normal." Callers know the auto attendant wasn't designed to help them. It was designed to help the company they are calling.

Cannes Lions is the Oscars of the advertising world. Advertisers from the world over descend on Cannes, France, to celebrate the most creative advertising of the year. Committees vote for their favorite advertisements; companies accept their awards, celebrate, and everyone goes home. There is little mention of impact or connection. In recent years, they have tried to pay homage with a nod to creative that is "effective," but they are vague in what effective means.

Making art and doing what most advertising companies do and producing what is often termed as "creative" are two entirely different things. Creative is focused on brand building. It is separate from the audience it is supposed to influence. Art forges connections. It builds relationships, and if done well, it will lift a brand with it. Advertising creative focuses on the brand, and art focuses on the audience. This distinction is one of the many reasons why traditional advertising is in such a steep decline.

WHERE ARE YOU HEADED?

"Would you tell me, please, which way I ought to go from here?"
"That depends a good deal on where you want to get to."
"I don't much care where."
"Then it doesn't matter which way you go."

—Lewis Carroll, *Alice in Wonderland*

Before you begin to apply the *Primal Storytelling* system, it is important to think deeply about what you are trying to achieve and to define your goals. What is it you want to accomplish with your content? Are you trying to build your website authority and traffic? Generate leads? Or maybe your goal is to build a community for your newest customers. Whatever your goal, it will inform your strategy and the tactics you develop to execute the strategy.

A few years ago, we were approached by a company to help them with their online reputation. They had been embroiled in a lawsuit, and an unflattering article was posted on a local news site about them. If you Googled their name, the article was one of the top results. Their own website was not even on the first page of the search results. It was a PR nightmare for them. They were sure they had lost business because of the article, and they were interested in moving the article off the first page of the search results.

When they engaged us, our goal was clear—help them dominate the first page of Google with their own brand content. It meant creating dozens of pages, ensuring they indexed properly, and most importantly, it meant creating valuable content that would be search engine friendly and do well on social media. They needed to build their domain authority for their entire website. They didn't get a lot of organic traffic and had virtually no social media presence. And to make it more difficult, they were located in New York City with enormous competition. It was a big undertaking.

This kind of goal requires a thoughtful strategy, and it takes time to put all of the pieces into place and for the pages to index and gain in popularity. After some discovery, we realized their target Tribes were deeply interested in architecture and construction. Many of them were also native New Yorkers and proud of the city. We opted to write a series of articles on the history of local buildings and interesting places around New York City that probably would not turn up on a usual tourist map. Most of the articles were long-form articles and included long-tail keywords and social media–friendly headlines. We also bought a number of small ads on social media for $5 to $100 to boost traffic to the articles we thought had the most appeal and encouraged readers to return to the site for more historical articles. The strategy paid off. After five months, their website was on the first page of Google, and after a year, they dominated searches that included different variations of their name. It was a big success against the goals we had set.

But then one day, while visiting their office, one of their partners approached me and asked, "Why aren't we generating more leads? We thought you were going to scale leads for the sales team."

I was taken by surprise. Lead generation was not one of the goals we were working on. It wasn't even on our radar. Early in the process, we had some cursory discussions with their marketing team about generating offers for landing pages, but nothing concrete. The focus was completely on reputation management and building their website authority. We could have accomplished both goals at the same time, but it would have required a different type of content strategy, and many more hours of work. Without identifying the second goal from the beginning, no strategy was executed to ensure its accomplishment. It was a complete failure on my part. I conducted a discovery session with them and completely missed it. I had interviewed the CEO, and then he had turned me over to the marketing team, but I never widened the conversation to other stakeholders in the organization.

I learned several lessons from the experience. I needed to do a better job of ensuring the goals of the marketing teams we work with aligned with the goals of their executive teams. Diverging goals among leadership teams, sales, and marketing are not unusual, but it is vital to have the conversations to ensure alignment and that everyone is headed in the same direction.

The experience also reinforced a truism for me—the strategy executed on behalf of a goal will dictate the results. If you plant tomatoes, don't be surprised at harvest time that you don't have watermelons. If you want to fish for trout, you will most likely bait your hook with worms or leeches and drop your hook and leave it near the bottom. But don't expect to catch pike that way! Pike like minnows. If you want to catch a pike, you need to bait your hook with a minnow and troll your boat, but don't expect to catch trout. Results correlate with strategy.

Brainstorm what is most important to your target market. Think about what may be important to them based on demographics and as you learn more about them, what is important to them based on their psychographic makeup. In the beginning, you will have to make some leaps based on your best guess of what is important to them until you gain some real-world data.

BACKWARD PLANNING

Accomplishing military objectives can be complex and confusing. Many different assets and resources are utilized in time and space, and understanding the correct sequencing of events can be difficult. As previously explained in the section on tribal data, military planners developed a planning process called backward planning as a way of simplifying their planning process. Backward planning helps planners quickly design a framework around their ideas. They envision an objective and begin asking the question, "What important task must occur just prior to this outcome?" They continue asking the question from the end objective until they reach the present time and the first steps that must be taken toward achieving the mission. If done well, the process reveals all the major events that must occur before accomplishing the objective with a tentative timeline and the resources necessary at each step along the way.

Backward planning also works well for planning marketing campaigns. After you have identified the goals of your campaign, you will choose one goal and ask the question, "What task must be accomplished just prior to accomplishing this goal?" The answer to the question will help identify the major tasks in the campaign. Keep asking the question for each of the major objectives in the campaign until you have a list of the major tasks. After your first pass through the campaign, identifying the large tasks, it's time to add time and resources to the project. Estimate how much time it will take to complete each major task and what resources and people are needed to accomplish it.

I like to use a whiteboard to plan out complex campaigns. If there is a hard deadline for the final goal, I write that goal with the date on the far right of the board and then work my way to the left, identifying the largest prior objectives that must be accomplished. After just a few minutes of work, you can quickly determine the major tasks and intermediate objectives that will lead to the accomplishment of the overall goal.

Marketing teams struggle with deciding what content to produce and how to do it. Most of them make the mistake of starting with their own products and services and starting to tell the world about them. They usually conduct a brainstorming session that starts with all the marketing material and brochures the company wrote about how great they are and ends with the decision to turn these into listicle blogs, social media posts, and other forms of corporate diarrhea. Most corporate content fails because it is lifeless, dry information that they try to disguise as useful content for their readers.

It can be helpful for marketing teams to understand the three types of content relevancy, as it pertains to their thing—what they actually do to serve clients. There is relevant content, semi-relevant content, and nonrelevant content.

Relevant content is what most marketers are already familiar with. It describes what you do, how you do it, and who you serve. It talks about the features and benefits and showcases the success stories of the company.

Semi-relevant content is not about you or your company. It is usually focused in some way on the industry or a parallel interest that is closely associated with what you do. As an example, an architectural firm might publish something on a new material that they want to incorporate into future designs. Or a manufacturer might publish about an emerging technology in manufacturing that could affect its customers.

Nonrelevant content has nothing to do with what your company does or its industry, but your target personas are interested in it. It can be a professional interest of some sort, but it can also be of personal interest and have nothing to do with work or the product at all. Nonrelevant content is the hardest for companies to embrace, but it has the biggest potential for long-term success.

All three types of content have one single purpose: engagement. Your content must be written for the target audience. It is very difficult for a company to create enough valuable content that will engage and hold an audience only talking about themselves. It is nearly impossible. Let's be very frank. Most businesses are boring. Not everyone is SpaceX and makes rockets that are going to help us migrate to Mars and save mankind from destruction. Most companies make something or provide a service that has a fairly narrow focus, and writing about everything interesting about that good or service might take five minutes or less, and then most of the world is bored to tears.

Semi-relevant and nonrelevant content broadens the horizon

of what is possible for a brand. An example of a brand that has done a good job of using semi-relevant and nonrelevant content is USAA. They are an insurance company, and there could hardly be anything more sleep-inducing than insurance. But they have done a great job of producing content that is valuable for their target markets—active-duty military, veterans, and their families.

Here are the headlines from just two articles from their blog:

"8 Fast Financial Tips for Military Recruits"

and

"How to Join the Military"

Neither article has anything to do with insurance. In fact, they are barely for their target market because you can't even do business with them until you are active duty or a veteran. They are targeting people who will one day possibly be in their target market. It is an intriguing strategy.

I have done an enormous amount of work with B-B companies, and sometimes the best results occur by taking semi-relevant and nonrelevant content ideas to their extreme. Not long ago, I engaged with a large manufacturing company that was trying to find a way to separate itself from the competition and get the attention of its target audience—engineers. More specifically, mechanical engineers.

Now, if you know any mechanical engineers, you know they tend to be highly educated, introverted, left-brained types. After several brainstorming sessions and some micro surveys, we produced an e-book written for young engineers just starting their careers, *The Fundamentals of Leadership*. It was a well-researched piece that performed exceptionally well and garnered positive feedback. It had absolutely nothing to do with our client's business. Do you think it separated them from every other manufacturer in their category? It certainly did.

When you are trying to determine what types of semi-relevant and nonrelevant content to produce, it helps to ask questions about your personas:

- What are they personally interested in?
- Are there any common interests among the group?
- What would help them improve their lives or career?
- Are there any cultural commonalities?
- Are there any frequent challenges they face as a group?
- Are there any frequently asked questions?

Many years ago, I served as the CEO of an IT services firm in New York City. IT services firms think of themselves as "managed services providers" (MSPs). We were a typical firm for the area and managed the IT systems for a host of different professional services companies, such as law firms, hedge funds, money managers, accountants, and the like. IT is one of the most boring industries imaginable to the target market. Very few people want to talk or read about cybersecurity, SEC compliance, or the latest Microsoft update. It can be a difficult category to produce content that will get even a passing glance from the target personas, and for a long time, we struggled to produce good content.

Take for example the persona we reviewed in Chapter 2, CFOs.

Many CFOs are responsible for the IT of their firms, and after meeting with many CFOs, I realized some CFOs struggled with how to manage IT people. The CFOs themselves rarely had a technical background, and many of them had graduated from college before computers or the internet were even widespread.

Our target Tribe's problem gave me an idea. I would write a book on how to help nonfinancial managers manage IT, and my book, *Cracking the IT Code: IT Management for Non-IT Managers*, was born. It was well-received by CFOs, and for years, I have used it to help generate leads for IT firms. In fact, even though I am not personally in IT anymore, it performed so well for our clients, I have been thinking about releasing an updated and expanded version of it.

Another example, this time of a B-C company was for a boutique hotel in New York City. They are a family-owned business that competes with thousands of other hotels, many of which are large chain hotels with massive marketing budgets. Before we began working with them, they struggled to get noticed online, and with their modest marketing budget, it seemed an uphill battle.

When we first took them on, I was nervous we wouldn't be able to generate stories that connected with their target audience. I visited the hotel several times, walked around their neighborhood, ate in their restaurant, and visited many of the parks, museums, and attractions nearby. Their hotel is not far from the Washington Arch in Washington Square Park, and I noticed the flocks of tourists in the area, and it got me thinking. What would someone who was visiting NYC for first time love to experience? And it hit me. People love to see celebrities. New York City is home to nearly as many celebrities as Hollywood, and who doesn't want to see a celebrity?

That idea eventually turned into the *Paparazzi's Guide to Greenwich Village*, which to date, has performed wonderfully. The guide was written as a way to improve a tourist's chances of seeing a celebrity while visiting NYC. It spoke directly to tourists who were visiting for the first time, and it was something unusual and original that none of the big chain hotels had on their website. To date, the guide has been downloaded thousands of times and garnered enormous attention for the hotel.

THE SHORT CONTENT TRAP

There is a persistent and widespread myth that content should be short and catchy. Often, companies will produce a flurry of 400- to 700-word listicles that they furiously post on different social media channels. If you ask them what the purpose of the content is, more often than not, they reply with nonsense like, "We are getting out there," or "We have to post every day to be relevant." The SEO "gurus" will tell you that you should be producing one to three blogs a week and posting to social media every day. That's what the search engines want to see to build your website authority, they say.

I cannot tell you how many times we have delivered a long-form piece of content to a client that is powerfully written and full of value, and their first response is, "It sure is long," or even worse, "I would never read something that long." Exactly, it IS long. It is long because that is how long it took to say something of value. And YOU are not the target persona. In fact, this wasn't written for you at all. No one cares what you think. We only care what the target personas think. Nothing else matters.

It is a myth that short content is in some way better than long-form content. Just because everyone is doing something doesn't make it correct or the right thing to do. Do you really believe posting fluffy little listicles is going to grow your brand or engage with your best-fit clients on a primal level? Will they love you for your next top ten list? Not likely.

If you are familiar with the Pareto principle, better known as the 80/20 rule, than you are familiar with the idea that some things produce more results than others. Not everything is of equal value, and SEO is more like a 95/5 ratio of effort to results. Meaning, great content will deliver 95 percent of the results and everything else about 5 percent.

Yes, you still need to have a technically sound website and follow SEO best practices, etc., but they in and of themselves won't have any effect if your content has no value, is boring, written for search engines, or all three.

Here is a revelation—most of the best-performing content on the internet is **long-form content**. And I don't mean slightly longer like 800 words. I mean *very* long. Two thousand words-plus is not unusual for good performing content. And there are many examples of content that is 10,000+ words performing admirably.

I know I sound like a heretic. "But…but…this is the age of attention deficit disorder. No one will read, watch, or listen to anything that is long!" you say.

No. It is not true. What is true is that no one will read, listen, or watch anything that is crap. Not even for one minute. They will stick around if you can produce something that is important to them, interesting, inspirational, or entertaining. But it has to be good, and it has to be valuable.

I used to be like most marketers. I wrote and helped produce hundreds of pieces of short-form content, but for a long time, I started to sense something was wrong. I saw the stats of our work across clients, and I knew some content was outperforming other content, but I couldn't quite put my finger on what the difference was. And then I attended a presentation in Boston by Tim Urban from the blog *Wait But Why*, www.waitbutwhy. com. Tim blew my mind.

For his blog, Tim wrote blog posts of 5,000, 10,000, even 20,000+ words that people read every word of and commented on. Some of his posts took more than eight hours a day for weeks to produce. And he broke every rule most content producers believe to be true. He wanted art in his blog, and so he hand drew stick figures and colored them himself. He wrote corny jokes and told stories about himself.

But his results speak for themselves. Many of his posts have gone viral, earning tens of thousands of likes, comments, and millions of views. If he had just one blog that went viral, you might be able to argue it was a fluke, but he has repeated his success over and over. Tim Urban's success in producing high-performing, long content is a clue to how a business can improve its content. Produce long-form content that is of interest and value for your target audience, and you will be rewarded with more social media engagement, organic traffic, and ultimately more leads and sales.

Another example of long-form content producing fantastic results is Tim Ferriss' website, www.fourhourworkweek.com. Some of his posts are almost excruciating in their detail and depth but take a look at the number of comments, shares, and the longevity of his posts. He delivers value with his posts, and value attracts an audience.

You might argue, "Tony, that is a bad example. Tim Ferriss is a celebrity author and podcaster." But he was writing long-form posts way before he was a national phenomenon. Tim knows his audience very well, and he is an interesting and entertaining guy. You might not like or agree with everything he writes, but you cannot dismiss his results. He has dozens of posts that have gone viral, and by building his website, one long post after another, he was able to use it to springboard to most everything else he is doing. I would argue one of the reasons he is a celebrity author and podcaster is because he took the time to provide value with long and exceptionally detailed posts.

I have never found a corporate blog that produced a viral hit with a listicle. If you find an example of one, please send it to me. I would love to see it, study it, and understand how, in a sea of dead content, it somehow rose above the rest. So far, all my arguments for long-form content have revolved around blogging, but podcasts and videos are following the same trend. On iTunes, James Altucher and Joe Rogan have shattered any doubt that long-form content performs well. Both of them create long episodes and have raving fans. Some of James's episodes are one-and-one-half to two hours long or even longer, and he has millions of followers. Joe Rogan's podcast and guests are very different from James's, but his episodes last as long as they last. In some episodes, Joe rambles, gets off-topic, and rants before finally coming back to anything relating to what the show is about, and his podcast is a huge hit. Joe is an engaging guy, and the length of his show is the last thing he is worried about. Some of these shows are very long while others are shorter, but none of them are five to ten minutes. They all stretch an hour or more.

On YouTube, the most followed channel of an individual is PewDiePie, with more than eighty-six million followers. He has varied the size of his videos over the years, but a quick glance through his posts, and you can see many high-performing videos that are more than an hour long and several that are two hours or more. His "short" videos tend to be around the ten-to-twenty-minute mark. And he is not the only one. If you search by nearly any subject, the trend is clear: long-form YouTube posts perform very well and invariably outperform short posts.

What is the right length for a piece of content? The length it takes to have a beginning, middle, and end *and* deliver all the value you possibly can and then a little more. The content should be as long as it takes to tell a compelling story that connects with your audience on a primal level. Steve Martin had profound advice not just for comedians, but for content producers. Your content should be "so good, they can't ignore you." And rarely does content that is that good come in a few paragraphs or a short little video.

There is an old saying full of timeless wisdom, "Stories aren't written. They are rewritten." And few things about writing are so true. The first draft of this book was horrible. It was beyond embarrassing. Large sections of it didn't make any sense and were so boring that they were the cure for insomnia. There were also many ideas in that first draft that didn't make it into the second draft. I threw out an entire section of the book—more than 15,000 words—that didn't contribute to the goal of creating an easy-to-use brand story template that gets results. The editing process is a somewhat humiliating and humbling experience.

Rewriting is a blessing in disguise. It gives you the opportunity to flush out ideas and winnow what works from what doesn't work. Rewrites help you focus your thoughts and ideas. I have a terrible habit of meandering around a subject and going off on tangents that don't have a lot of relevance to the thought at hand, and it makes my initial drafts very difficult to follow. The rewriting and editing processes are the real work of creating something valuable. They are your friend. Everyone focuses on the first draft, but it is the first 10 percent of the writing process. The hard and arguably most valuable work is all the work you do after the first draft.

It is a rare occurrence when the form of a first draft will survive editing and rewriting. Authors need the space of the first draft to get everything they needed to say on a subject out into the world, and then they refine their ideas. One of the most damaging myths in art is the idea of a fully formed piece being completed in a short amount of time and achieving perfection from the start.

I personally have never been able to accomplish it, nor have any of the dozens of writers I have worked with over the years. Fully formed first drafts are just not how art (or at least solidly competent writing) is created. As a brand writer, it is unlikely that you are going to create the brand version of *The Old Man and the Sea*, but it is important to take the writing and editing seriously enough that you follow the same process as Hemingway.

Write, rewrite, edit, and rewrite some more! Art requires iteration and refinement. It doesn't leap from the brain onto the canvas fully formed. It is coached out a little at a time. Hemingway is famous for having written and rewritten the ending to *Farewell to Arms* at least thirty-nine times. If Hemingway, one of the greatest writers of all time, saw the value in iteration, it only follows that we embrace it.

One rule I always enforce is that no one is allowed to edit their own work. I write every day and have published hundreds of articles, blogs, white papers, and two books, and I still do not edit my own work. It is just too hard, and your mind cannot see your own mistakes. When you labor over something intensely, your brain begins to filter out what is actually written. It knows what it wants to say, and when you read something you wrote, your brain will fill in words that don't exist and jump over words that do exist. It will literally skip over obvious mistakes on the paper and correct them for you. So, when you read it, it sounds perfect, and then someone else reads it, and they will struggle to understand what you are saying.

There are three types of editing most companies will find valuable:

1. Developmental editing
2. Copyediting
3. Proofreading

Developmental editing is the most difficult of the three and the most valuable. A developmental editor reviews a piece, but not for its structural and technical correctness. The developmental editor is focused on the story, clarity, and quality of the writing. Does it accomplish its purpose? Does it make sense? Where are the holes in the structure?

The developmental editor is like a coach of a star athlete. She is trying to draw the absolute best work out of the writer: to have a deep discussion about the work without ego or premise and help the writer to decide where to focus for the next iteration of rewrites. The developmental editor's job is to nudge the work toward excellence.

The copyedit is focused on the use of language. Does the piece follow the rules of written English or at least break the rules with foresight and purpose? Not everyone can be a copy editor. It takes a very specialized understanding of language and experience and real focus. I, for one, am a terrible copy editor. I read right through mistakes.

The final type of edit is a proofread. It is most efficiently done by someone with some distance from the project, and they are looking for glaring errors. If you have ever found a mistake in a professionally done book, advertisement, or other publication, it is invariably because they skipped this step due to being in a hurry.

Other than poor editing, the most common mistake I see in the author's work is poor structure. They mix ideas and concepts in a hodgepodge that is not simple or easy to follow. Focus on one single idea per piece. The singular focus will help retain the reader's interest and make it easier to write. Complexity makes everything more difficult.

INSIGHT

Planning is a shortcut to success. A content marketing program with a detailed action plan will almost always outperform a haphazard program that depends on last minute, "just get it out the door" thinking. Don't be afraid to produce long-form content that covers a subject in-depth. If it is well done, informative, and targeted, it will have a great chance of performing better than most short pieces.

CAUTION

Don't overthink it. Nothing will be perfect. Make a plan and start executing on it. Don't wait for inspiration or a lot more data. Gather just enough data to get started and begin. You can make changes as you move forward.

KEY QUESTIONS

1. Am I holding back from publishing my best work because I am afraid of being judged?
2. Does our content marketing plan include at least ninety days of content?
3. Is my content short because I think short content outperforms long content, or is it short because that fits the message?

CHAPTER NINE

PRIMAL STORYTELLING IN ACTION

> **The Primal Storytelling Formula:**
>
> **Tribe + Urges and Emotions + Story = Primal Story**

Tribal Persona:	Primal Urges/Emotions
Demographics:	**Urges:** food, shelter, clothing, safety, protection, sex, curiosity, significance, spirituality
Psychographics:	**Emotions:** curiosity, fear, envy, lust, love, excitement, nostalgia, surprise
Story Structure:	**Value Stories:**
Narrative Voice:	1.
Archetype:	2.
	3.
Plots:	
	Origin Story:
	Vision Story:
	Transformation Story:

Creating content is a lot like baking a cake. The base ingredients (flour, water, sugar, and baking powder) are always the same, but variations in the rest of the ingredients, added flavors, and decorations result in a nearly infinite number of different cakes.

For content creators, the number of story structures, urges, and emotions are limited, but your creativity is unbound. As your experience with applying the formula grows, so will your ability to create extraordinary original content.

To create your plan, follow the formula in order. Begin with defining the Tribe. Review the process described in Chapter 2 for gathering demographic and psychographic data on your target Tribe and implement it. It is the foundation for everything else that follows. If you do a good job gaining an understanding of your Tribe, everything that follows is easier. I included some Tribe examples at the end of this section. Use them as a model to create your own Tribes.

Next choose two to three Primal Urges and a couple of emotions to focus on for your preliminary campaigns. Ask yourself one guiding question, "How do I want the customer to feel when they buy?" Your goal is to evoke this emotion with your content over time. You are going to weave these emotions and urges into your stories and as they are consumed. If done well, they will help connect your brand with the Tribe.

Finally, you will begin to create story lines by choosing a narrative voice, archetypes, and at least one plot structure to get started. Keep in mind, at the beginning of the program most everything is an experiment to help you understand what will connect most strongly with your Tribe. Most brands can benefit from all four story types: origin, vision, transformation, and value. But for some brands, the origin and vision stories are too difficult to get through company bureaucracy or don't make sense for the situation. In those cases, focus on the transformation and value stories. The transformation stories will help the Tribe understand what it is you do for them and what it looks like before, during, and after working with your brand, and it will help them connect with you and your sales process.

TRIBE EXAMPLES
EXAMPLE 1: BUSINESS TO BUSINESS (B-B)

The first example is the same company I mentioned in Chapter 6. It was a manufacturing firm that wanted to connect with young engineers who could influence future projects. They were in business for more than seventy-five years and realized many of the individuals they did the most business with were nearing the end of their careers. They wanted to target younger engineers just out of college and in the first few years of their career.

They had a large email list, but with poor segmentation. They did not know who in their list fit the correct demographic.

Tribe: Level I Engineer

Include a picture of a member of your tribe.	
	Demographics:
	College educated. 22–29 Years old. First 1–3 years of work. Lack of real-world experience. Understands how engineering works but is lacking many advanced details and has not yet established a core niche or expertise. Wants to advance his career. This is a male dominated industry with little female representation.
Engineering Eric	

Psychographics: A junior engineer who is focused on not making any big mistakes that will get him fired. Wants to learn as much as possible right now to make a big contribution as fast as possible.

Interests: He has many varied interests typical of the age group: travel, sports, video games, athletics, as well as job-related interests, such as science, technology, futurism, robotics, etc.

Fears: Eric is anxious to make an impact on the world but is also hesitant to take too many chances and make a big mistake. He understands he needs to work toward his professional engineering license, but realizes many engineers never earn it because the requirements are very stringent. He would like to advance his career and hopes to pay off his student debt.

Pain Points: Trying to learn advanced engineering concepts and how business works. Learning leadership lessons. Creativity. Maintaining work-life balance.

Primal Urges

- Protection
- Security
- Significance

Value Themes

After conducting our initial research and brainstorming sessions, we came up with two separate value themes for them:

- The first was that many new engineers recognize they need to gain leadership skills. During college, they worked mainly as individuals and as a team member on group projects but have little experience as leaders.
- The second value theme came after surveying engineering managers and their desire for new hires to be more creative overall in their approach to problem-solving.

We used the two value themes to produce dozens of lead magnets, articles, and social media posts. The content was used to increase social media interactions, website traffic, and lead nurturing.

The campaigns resulted in thousands of engineers self-identifying and **more than 2,500 e-book downloads!** The company's website traffic, blog post views, and time on site also increased. The content was of such high quality that the company successfully used it in advertisements in trade journals and on social media. The campaign is directly attributable to several revenue-generating projects, which was not the original goal, but a welcome side effect.

EXAMPLE 2: BUSINESS TO BUSINESS (B-B)

The second example for B-B is for a SaaS company targeting oral surgery clinics. Their software program was designed to help clinics run more efficiently and profitably. They did not have a list or social media following, and they were struggling to create content that was relevant for their target audiences. We created multiple tribal personas for them. For this example, we are including just the primary persona of Oral Surgeons.

Tribe: Oral Surgeons (Clinicians)

Include a picture of a member of your tribe.	
	Demographics:
	There are more than 9,000 oral surgeons in the US. They are found in every region of the US with concentrations in urban areas. Oral surgeons are one of the highest paid sub-specialities of dentist with the average surgeon earning $500K+ with regional variation. Because of the extensive education requirements (four years undergraduate, four years graduate, four to six years residency), oral surgeons begin practice around the age of thirty-one to thirty-three and the average age of all surgeons is fifty-plus. Oral surgeons in the US are predominantly men even though the trend for dental professionals skews female.
Oral Surgeon Oscar	

Psychographics: Oral surgeons are a sub-class of elite professionals within the dentistry field. Many oral surgeons do not think of themselves as dentists even though all oral surgeons must be dentists first, and then they specialize in oral surgery.

Interests: As might be expected, oral surgeons have many of the same interests as a cross section of the general population, but because they are older, they tend to gravitate toward hobbies such as golf, jogging, fine dining, and other generalized pursuits. Many oral surgeons are members of the American

Association of Oral and Maxillofacial Surgeons (AAOMS), the American Dental Association, and in some cases the Society of OMS Administrators.

Fears: Oral surgeons who are also practice owners have many fears related to running a small business. They are afraid of the reputational risk and business of potential lawsuits and HR issues. Many surgeons would just like to practice medicine and let others run the practice. They would like to increase their earnings but are constrained by time and their ability to keep up with the administrative burdens of the field. Government regulation in the industry is extremely heavy and expensive.

Pain Points: Many oral surgeons are married with families and achieving a balanced life can be a challenge. In addition, mothers struggle to manage raising children with the life of a practice, and it is one of the contributing factors to only a small number of surgeons who are women. For some practice owners, creating operational excellence is difficult because they are also delivering patient care. For those who are nearing retirement, the pain points of selling their practice and maximizing a lifetime of investment becomes a pain point.

Primal Urges
- Safety
- Security
- Significance

Value Themes
We created two separate value themes for them:

- The first is that they are a light in the darkness for improving practice management. It not only can improve the performance and profitability of the practice, but it can also improve a doctor's life.
- Second, by systematizing practice management software, firms could increase profits and improve customer satisfaction while the surgeons enjoyed a higher standard of life.

The two value themes led to lead magnets tied to practice efficiency and many blogs that targeted the oral surgeons and their staff. The lead magnets were used with webinars, social media posts, and social media ads targeted toward oral surgeons that generated a solid flow of leads and that then doubled website traffic and page views in less than ninety days.

EXAMPLE 3: BUSINESS TO CONSUMER (B-C)

The next example was developed for more than one client who wanted to connect with Montana expatriates. Montana is a great place to live and raise a family, but it has limited career opportunities. Many new graduates leave the state in search of work only to find they want to return when it is time to have a family. They remember how great it was growing up in Montana, the high quality of life, as well as having a desire to be closer to the family they left behind, and they begin the process of moving back to Montana.

Tribe: Montana Expatriates

Include a picture of a member of your tribe.	
	Demographics:
	Rita and Rob live far away from their families and they are thinking about moving back to Montana to raise a family. One or both of them graduated from a Montana university, and is a native Montanan. After graduation they couldn't find a good paying job in Montana or just wanted to try living in another state and moved out of state.
	The average age of a first-time mother in the US is ~twenty-six years old. The trend is for women to have a few children later in life than previous generations, and Rita puts off having children for longer than the the average because of uncertainty.
Rita and Rob Return	

Psychographics: Rita and Rob are having second thoughts about moving away from Montana. They are in a different place in life than when they first moved away and now appreciate Montana's quiet, family-friendly environment. They want to raise their kids in an area in Montana that is relatively close to family, has good schools, and good jobs nearby.

Interests: As might be expected, Rita and Rob have many of the same interests as a cross section of the general population. For our purposes, we are focused on their interest in jobs, schools, and affordability of housing on their return to Montana.

Fears: They are afraid they will not be able to find good jobs or affordable housing when they return to Montana.

Pain Points: Living far from family; job searches; affordable housing.

EXAMPLE 4: BUSINESS TO CONSUMER (B-C)

The fourth example is one of the Tribes we developed for the *Primal Storytelling* academy. In the beginning of developing *Primal Storytelling*, I was unsure who I would teach it to until I tested the messaging and had some real interest from the newest generation of marketers to have a foundation to build on.

Tribe: Marketing Coordinators

Include a picture of a member of your tribe.	
	Demographics:
	Julia is a marketer in the first few years of her career. She is eighteen to twenty-five, a high school graduate, and maybe a collage graduate, and more likely than not single. She is often tasked with creating social media posts for her company or if she is inside an agency, for her clients. She has a feel for how social media works, but she has never grown a large social media following. She is eager to learn more about digital marketing to improve the results of her clients and get promoted and further her career. She has never been formally trained in social media. Her job titles vary: marketing coordinator, social media coordinator, inbound coordinator, etc.
Julia	

Psychographics: Julia is energetic, excited about her career, and she's eager to learn new things. She is also wary about wasting her time with nonsense. There are many so-called marketing, copywriting, and other such courses in the world, but there are few that train you in a content creation process.

Interests: As might be expected, Julia has many interests in her personal life shared by the average eighteen- to twenty-five-year-old as well as her career interests in all things digital marketing.

Fears: Not having the right skills to get ahead; buying a course that is a waste of time.

Pain Points: She does have a formal process for creating content, but has no story structures; available sources of learning are limited.

AFTERWORD

The future of marketing is not hard to predict. The rate of technological change will continue to increase. Virtual reality, augmented reality, and likely an emergent technology that hasn't been invented yet, will surface, and alter some of the ways content can be accessed online and in the home. AI may even assist writers in creating content, or take over the task completely. It will all be very exciting.

What won't change are the people themselves. They will still love stories like they always have. They will still be the same flawed, emotional beings they were when Gronk first sat around the fire, telling his story of killing a saber-toothed tiger. Their primal urges and emotions will also be the same, and they will continue to buy emotionally and then attempt to justify their decisions with logic.

The structure of stories and how they connect with the human language will also remain constant. Algorithms may help content creators analyze emerging trends to aid in crafting the best stories for the moment, but the stories themselves will not suddenly shift to some new, unheard-of structure. All of the most successful story structures have more likely than not already been invented, and the same structures will continue to be successful in the future.

One thing will change, and the marketing world is just now starting to wake up to this new reality. Audiences will grow increasingly immune to brand advertising that is blatantly promotional and has no connecting story or message. There is just too much of it. The world is awash in advertising and as a defense mechanism, the mind must tune out the noise. Brands that don't adapt to this new reality will face becoming ignored and irrelevant.

People have nearly infinite choices, and those channels that do not bombard them with interruptive advertising, and instead tell authentic stories that touch on the emotions and primal urges that make us human will thrive. Storytelling will become even more important in the future because people want more human connection and less automation. Brands will be forced to package their goods and services within content that people choose to consume. Brand storytellers who understand the primal nature of their audiences and are experts in the structure of stories will be in hot demand for many years to come.

ADDITIONAL RESOURCES

The one point I hope I made clear is that even though technology will change and evolve, the heart of humanity and our love of stories will remain the same. That doesn't mean telling the right story at the right time for a business is easy. In fact, it is quite difficult. And that is why I created a community of what I like to think of as *Primal Storytellers* at www.primalstorytelling. com. It is a place to gain inspiration from other storytellers on what was successful for them, and to help one another. As part of the community and email list, you will receive invitations for when I do the occasional free "Ask Me Anything" live video call. I try to answer questions and offer advice for those in the process of implementing *Primal Storytelling* into their business. There are also a number of planning tools and guides that will help you with planning and implementation.

I look forward to hearing your story!

www.primalstorytelling.com/bookresources

You can contact me at anthony@primalstorytelling.com

Or follow me on social media:

YouTube: Anthony L. Butler

Instagram: @Anthonylbutler

LinkedIn: https://www.linkedin.com/in/
anthony-butler-964b404/

ABOUT THE AUTHOR

ANTHONY BUTLER is the founder of the digital marketing agency Can-Do Ideas and the creator of the *Primal Storytelling*™ content system. He is a highly regarded expert in brand storytelling and digital marketing. Anthony graduated from the United States Military Academy at West Point, and the US Army Ranger School. He commanded an infantry company during the invasion of Iraq and is a recipient of the bronze star medal. He is an avid martial artist and is a black belt in Brazilian Jiu-Jitsu. He currently resides in Montana with his wife and two sons.

NOTES

INTRODUCTION

1   "Total Number of Websites," Internet Live Stats, accessed July 7, 2022, https://www. internetlivestats.com/total-number-of-websites/.

CHAPTER ONE

1   Kevin Kelly, *The Inevitable: Understanding the 12 Technological Forces That Will Shape Our Future* (New York, NY: Penguin Books, 2016), 6.

2   Yuval Noah Harari, *Sapiens: A Brief History of Humankind* (New York, NY: Harper Perennial, 2018).

3   Steven Pinker, *The Blank Slate: The Modern Denial of Human Nature* (New York, NY: Penguin, 2019).

4   Robert Wright, *The Moral Animal: Why We Are the Way We Are: The New Science of Evolutionary Psychology* (London: Abacus, 1996).

5   Alan S. Cowen and Dacher Keltner, "Self-report Captures 27 Distinct Categories of Emotion Bridged by Continuous Gradients," *PNAS* 114, no. 38 (September 5, 2017): E7900-E7909, https:// doi.org/10.1073/pnas.1702247114; "The Emotions Evoked by Video," Amazon Web Services, accessed April 16, 2021, https://s3-us-west-1.amazonaws.com/emogifs/map.html#.

6   Jonathan Gottschall, *The Storytelling Animal: How Stories Make Us Human* (Boston, MA: Houghton Mifflin Harcourt, 2013); Lisa Cron, *Wired for Story: The Writer's Guide to Using Brain Science to Hook Readers from the First Sentence* (Berkeley, CA: Ten Speed Press, 2012).

7   Joshua Foer, *Moonwalking with Einstein: The Art and Science of Remembering Everything* (New York, NY: Penguin Books, 2011).

8   Maryam Mohsin, "10 YouTube Statistics That You Need to Know in 2021," *Oberlo* (blog), March 25, 2021, https://www.oberlo.com/blog/youtube-statistics#.

CHAPTER TWO

1   Harari, *Sapiens.*

2   Malcolm Gladwell, *The Tipping Point: How Little Things Can Make a Big Difference* (Boston, MA: Little, Brown, 2006), 17. British Anthropologist Robin Dunbar theorized the size of the species' neocortex correlates to the largest group the species will work in, and humans are the largest topping out at about 150 people. He did a study of tribes and used the examples of the military and Hutterites who all limited membership to 150 members because that was the limit that individuals can maintain social relationships of any kind of value.

3   Cohen, F. (n.d.). *Isolation in penal settings: The isolation-restraint paradigm.* Retrieved April 19, 2021, from https://openscholarship.wustl.edu/law_journal_law_policy/vol22/iss1/23/

4   Fred Reichheld, *The Ultimate Question: Driving Good Profits and True Growth* (Boston, MA: Harvard Business School Press, 2006).

5   Linda and Charlie Bloom, "The Bandwagon Effect," *Psychology Today*, August 11, 2017, https://www.psychologytoday.com/us/blog/stronger-the-broken-places/201708/the-bandwagon-effect.

6   Harry Piotr, "Apple – Think Different – Full Version," YouTube video, 1:09, September 30, 2013, https://www.youtube.com/watch?v=5sMBhDv4sik.

7   Sam Costello, "This Is the Number of iPods Sold All-Time," Livewire, first accessed March 10, 2021, https://www.lifewire.com/number-of-ipods-sold-all-time-1999515; archived at *Wayback Machine* (https://web.archive.org) capture dated March 13, 2021.

8   Kevin Kelly, "1,000 True Fans," *The Technium* (blog), KK.org, accessed April 19, 2021, https://kk.org/thetechnium/1000-true-fans.

9   Charles Duhigg, "How Companies Learn Your Secrets – *The New York Times Magazine*," CharlesDuhigg.com, accessed April 19, 2021, https://charlesduhigg.com/new-york-times-magazine/.

10   Charles Duhigg, *The Power of Habit: Why We Do What We Do in Life and Business* (Toronto: Anchor Canada, 2012).

11   United States Census Bureau, "Total Population in the United States," Data.census.gov, accessed April 19, 2021, https://data.census.gov/cedsci/map?q=Total+Population+in+the+United+States&g=0100000US.04000.001&tid=ACSDP1Y2018.DP05&vintage=2018&layer=VT_2018_040_00_PP_D1&cid=DP05_0001E.

CHAPTER THREE

1   Melanie L. Glocker et al., "Baby Schema in Infant Faces Induces Cuteness Perception and Motivation for Caretaking in Adults," *Ethology* 115 no. 3 (March 2009): 257–263, https://doi.org/10.1111%2Fj.1439-0310.2008.01603.x.

2   Glocker et al., "Baby Schema."

3   "Stories of Sacrifice," Congressional Medal of Honor Society, accessed April 19, 2021, https://www.cmohs.org/recipients. We surveyed the medal of honor write-ups for those who paid the ultimate price by covering a grenade with their body. WW II = 44, Korean War = 22. Vietnam War = 80, Afghanistan = 2, Iraq = 3. Total: 151.

4   Brian Mustanski, *The Sexual Continuum* (blog), *Psychology Today*, accessed April 19, 2021, https://www.psychologytoday.com/us/blog/the-sexual-continuum. The stats used are median thoughts per day taken during a self-report study conducted by Dr. Terri D. Fisher, Professor of Psychology at The Ohio State University at Mansfield.

5   Sage Lazzaro, "9 Crazy Stats That Prove We Watched a Whole Lot of Porn in 2016," *Observer*, January 6, 2017, https://observer.com/2017/01/pornhub-stats-data-2016.

CHAPTER FOUR

1   Daniel Gilbert, *Stumbling on Happiness* (London, UK: Vintage Books, 2006).

2   Paul Eckman, "Universal Emotions: What Are Emotions?" Paul Ekman Group, accessed April 22, 2021, https://www.paulekman.com/universal-emotions.

3   Alan S. Cowen and Dacher Keltner, "Self-Report Captures 27 Distinct Categories of Emotion Bridged by Continuous Gradients," *PNAS* 114, no. 38 (September 5, 2017): E7900-E7909, https://doi.org/10.1073/pnas.1702247114; "The Emotions Evoked by Video."

4   Taryn Hillin, "So Guilt Isn't an Emotion?" *Splinter*, June 22, 2015, https://splinternews.com/so-guilt-isnt-an-emotion-1793848574.

5   George Tannenbaum, "To Writers. (The Rare Ones Who Write.)," *Ad Aged* (blog), April 5, 2019, http://adaged.blogspot.com/2019/04/to-writers-rare-ones-who-write.html.

CHAPTER FIVE

1   Ferris Jabr, "The Story of Storytelling," *Harper's Magazine*, March 2019, https://harpers.org/archive/2019/03/the-story-of-storytelling.

2   Jabr, "The Story of Storytelling."

3   Molika Ashford, "How Are Memories Stored in the Brain?" *Live Science*, August 31, 2010, https://www.livescience.com/32798-how-are-memories-stored-in-the-brain.html.

4   Frances A. Yates, *The Art of Memory* (London: Routledge & K. Paul, 1966), 1–2. I also found *Moon Walking with Einstein* by Joshua Foer (Penguin Books, 2012) and Timothy Ferriss's description of the Loci method in his book, *The 4-Hour Chef* (New Harvest, 2012) to be helpful and entertaining. I spent a few months learning the Loci method as well as the major system for memorizing strings of numbers. After some practice, I was able to memorize a deck of cards in just under ten minutes and dramatically improved my ability to recall people's names. I will never be a memory champion, but I did feel like it increased my ability to focus.

5   Robert B. Cialdini, *Influence: The Psychology of Persuasion* (New York, NY: Harper Business, 2006).

6   Michael Pollan, "Michael Pollan – Exploring the Frontiers of Psychedelics (#365)," March 21, 2019, in *The Tim Ferriss Show*, hosted by Tim Ferriss, podcast, 1:38:58, https://tim.blog/2019/03/21/michael-pollan-sxsw.

7   Robert J. Szczerba, "Mixed Martial Arts and the Evolution of John McCain," *Forbes*, April 3, 2014, https://www.forbes.com/sites/robertszczerba/2014/04/03/mixed-martial-arts-and-the-evolution-of-john-mccain/#246dd3642d59.

CHAPTER SIX

1   SpaceX, "Making Life Multiplanetary," YouTube video, September 29, 2017, 43:28, https://www.youtube.com/watch?v=tdUX3ypDVwI.

2   Rheana Murray, "Subway Commercial Spokesman Jared Fogle Marks 15 Years of Turkey Subs and Keeping the Weight Off," *New York Daily News*, June 9, 2013, https://www.nydailynews.com/life-style/health/jared-subway-guy-marks-15-years-turkey-subs-article-1.1365511.

3   Jonathan Maze, "Why Subway Is Facing a Crisis," Restaurant Business Online, January 19, 2018, https://www.restaurantbusinessonline.com/financing/why-subway-facing-crisis.

4   Deborah Turness, "A Note from Deborah Turness," NBC News PR, February 10, 2015, http://press.nbcnews.com/2015/02/10/a-note-from-deborah-turness.

5   Jason Davis, "A Million People in 40 to 100 Years: SpaceX Unveils Plan to Colonize Mars," The Planetary Society, September 27, 2016, http://www.planetary.org/blogs/jason-davis/2016/20160927-spacex-unveils-mars-plans.html.

CHAPTER SEVEN

1   Martha Lagace, "The Consumer Appeal of Underdog Branding," Harvard Business School – Working Knowledge, September 13, 2010, https://hbswk.hbs.edu/item/the-consumer-appeal-of-underdog-branding.

2   Rupal Parekh, "After 50 Years, Avis Drops Iconic 'We Try Harder' Tagline," *Ad Age*, August 27, 2012, https://adage.com/article/news/50-years-avis-drops-iconic-harder-tagline/236887.

3   Krystal Overmyer, "The Psychological Appeal of Underdog Brand Positioning," *Skyword*, May 2, 2018, https://www.skyword.com/contentstandard/the-psychological-appeal-of-underdog-brand-positioning/.

4   Casey Neistat, "Make It Count," YouTube video, 4:37, April 9, 2012, https://www.youtube.com/watch?v=WxfZkMm3wcg.

5   Josh Jones, "The (Urban) Legend of Ernest Hemingway's Six-Word Story: 'For Sale, Baby Shoes, Never Worn.'," Open Culture, March 24, 2015, http://www.openculture.com/2015/03/the-urban-legend-of-ernest-hemingways-six-word-story.html.

6   Ram Trucks, "Farmer | Ram Trucks," YouTube video, 2:02, February 3, 2013, https://www.youtube.com/watch?v=AMpZoTGjbWE.

Made in the USA
Las Vegas, NV
18 December 2022

63423465R00136

PRIMAL STORYTELLING